"Ralph was a teammate others paved the way for me and many African Americans to follow. Ralph was a great athlete who could make a tackler miss him in a phone booth. But Ralph is also a great man. I thoroughly enjoyed reading his book. *One of the First* reveals the truth that with commitment, perseverance, and faith, you can overcome any obstacle in life, including racism."

— OZZIE NEWSOME, NFL HALL OF FAME TIGHT END AND FIRST AFRICAN AMERICAN GENERAL MANAGER IN THE NFL

"I was captivated reading *One of the First*. It was like being a spectator watching Ralph play the game of life —as he outruns, out jumps, and stiff-arms discrimination, segregation, the KKK, and various other forms of bigotry. Through challenges and setbacks, hurts and disappointments, Ralph's class and character shine brightly. He was never compromised by hatred or bitterness for those who mistreated him. Ralph is a man who loves other human beings because he knows that to hate is a waste of time. Readers will not be able to put this book down."

— DR. KELVIN CROOM, SENIOR PASTOR, COLLEGE HILL BAPTIST CHURCH

"With his new book, *One of the First*, Ralph has drawn out tremendous wisdom from his personal life, addressing some issues that are uncomfortable. He does not point fingers, but he does teach some very valuable lessons about racial issues and about persevering through challenges. A must read for everyone."

— WENDELL HUDSON, FIRST AFRICAN AMERICAN SCHOLARSHIP ATHLETE AT THE UNIVERSITY OF ALABAMA

"Ralph has displayed great courage throughout his life as he fought for the cause of integration, and that courage is on full display in *One of the First*. While Ralph achieved many firsts, I appreciate in particular that he fought for the right of Black athletes to join a fraternity. His perseverance has led to a host of other Black athletes following in his footsteps."

— CHRISTOPHER SPENCER, FACULTY ADVISOR, BETA ETA CHAPTER OF OMEGA PSI PHI FRATERNITY, INC.

"In *One of the First*, Ralph gives us an inside look at how it was for him to be one of the first to break many racial barriers. I knew there was something special about Ralph when I first met him in Bryant Hall in 1971. I'm proud to call Ralph my friend, and I'm also proud of him for writing this book. Everyone who reads it will be inspired by his wisdom, his class, and the way he has lived his life. Thank you, Ralph!"

— RICKY DAVIS, SPORTS AGENT AND FORMER
NFL DEFENSIVE BACK

ONE OF THE FIRST

LESSONS I LEARNED WHILE OVERCOMING THE CHALLENGES OF INTEGRATION

RALPH STOKES

with

CHRIS MCKINNEY

Foreword by

SYLVESTER CROOM

CALLED WRITERS
CHRISTIAN PUBLISHING

COPYRIGHT

CONTENTS

It has often been said that football builds character. I am of the opinion that football played under Coach Paul 'Bear' Bryant revealed character. Players were put into situations that forced them, as he put it, "to show what your mama and daddy taught you."

So it was with Ralph Stokes. In 1971, I had the privilege of joining Ralph, along with three other Black players, in being one of the first five Black players to join the University of Alabama football team. As one of the most sought-after running backs in the nation, Ralph arrived with fans, coaches, and teammates anticipating that he would be a key figure, helping lead the Crimson Tide to multiple national titles.

Ralph quickly learned that life presents unexpected challenges, and that our commitment often gets tested. His response to the challenges he faced while playing football at Alabama will leave you inspired.

Fortunately for all of us, Ralph did not stop rising to meet challenges. Throughout his life, he has broken many barriers, from the world of football, to the business world, to the world of golf. Ralph consistently persevered through biases, blatant racism, and other challenges, paving the way for those who came after him.

Ralph has proven to be a winner where it counts the most —in life. I am proud to call Ralph Stokes my teammate and my friend.

May his story inspire you to greater heights.

— SYLVESTER CROOM, FIRST AFRICAN
AMERICAN HEAD FOOTBALL COACH IN THE
SOUTHEASTERN CONFERENCE

INTRODUCTION

Writing a book about my experiences was not something that really ever came to my mind. A few people had suggested it to me over the years and most recently, my friend John Covington urged me to consider that my story could be helpful for others. Other people seemed to agree with John, and though I was still somewhat reluctant, I decided to move forward with the project.

Even after we started the book, I still wasn't sure of the exact purpose. I told the people involved that if the book could somehow help others—even just one person—it would be worth the effort.

Now I believe that God planned this moment a long time ago. All of the experiences in my life seem to have been designed to lead me here—to the point of being able to encourage others by sharing my stories.

I hope these stories inspire you to persevere through life's challenges so that you can reach your full potential.

1

THE END OF SEGREGATED ATHLETICS

From as far back as I can remember, I wanted to be just like my dad's incredible athletes. Well before I was ever born, Frank Stokes Sr. owned multiple businesses. Dad was a barber, picking up the skill during his time in the military, so of course he owned his own barber shop. He had one or two other barbers working in there at any given time. There was the washateria, also known as a laundromat, which was located a few neighborhoods over from where we lived.

He owned a corner grocery store called "The Sweet Shop." And then there were a few other businesses I won't comment on. But suffice it to say, he loved business. In fact when he was 75 years old, he tried to buy a gas station, thinking he still had what it took to run a business. He probably did, but we all got together and talked him out of it.

There was no talking him out of anything for the majority of his life. While owning and operating those businesses, Dad also worked full time as the head butcher for Swift Packing Company. His wages were some of the highest wages available to laborers of that day and time. So that afforded him a little extra money to invest. And invest he did.

My father was a businessman through and through, and growing up as the son of a perpetual entrepreneur was a blessing in more ways than one. For example, coming up in that type of environment gave me plenty of chances to learn about business. Dad always assigned us different responsibilities in his businesses, so my siblings and I developed strong work ethics and learned many important skills.

One of my dad's most frequent sayings was, "Do right and right will follow you." He was very earnest about preparing us for life. We learned about the responsibility of opening and closing businesses, purchasing and sales, inventory management, community relations, equipment and building maintenance, and a host of other valuable skills.

But one of the most important blessings of being the son of a serial entrepreneur was that it fueled my passion for sports. You see, my dad also owned a Negro league baseball team called The Montgomery Red Legs. Now before you decide that I must have been rich growing up, I should tell you that owning a Negro league team back then didn't take very much capital.

The Montgomery Red Legs circa 1962

This was not a big-time team with well-known players. There were several Negro league teams in Montgomery, Alabama, at that time. Our team got to play against teams like the Birmingham Black Barons, where Willie Mays played. We also played against the team in Mobile, Alabama, where Hank Aaron had played. But getting into the major leagues was still pretty tough for Black players in those days, so there were very few who actually made it and went on to become famous.

To get started owning a team, you really just had to buy all of the uniforms and equipment and then be able to pay a per game fee to someone to manage the team. As I recall, Dad basically got to keep money from concession sales in exchange for his investment and efforts.

The big benefit for my older brother Theron and me was being around all of those amazing Black athletes. Many of them had also played football in high school and college. We

17

wanted to be just like them, and they inspired us to pursue sports passionately. Theron was a little older and a little stronger than me, so he was another source of inspiration. I was motivated to be just as big and as fast and as strong as he was.

But like most younger brothers, I also wanted to beat my older brother. It's hard to be perpetually a little bit smaller and weaker than the person you compete against on a daily basis. We were outside playing sports every chance we got. If we weren't running a race, we were playing baseball. If we weren't doing those things, we were playing football in the schoolyard across the street.

Theron was a competitor. He had a very competitive spirit, so he never let up on me. We both tried our best to duplicate what we saw my dad's players doing. They could run. They could hit. They could throw. And we wanted to do it just like them.

At an early age, it was apparent that I had strong athletic ability. My first foray into organized sports was playing for my elementary school's football team. Back then, youth leagues were not nearly as well developed as they are now. There was only one team for all of the elementary school kids, so when I began playing in the 3rd grade, I was on the field with 4th graders. And 5th graders. And 6th graders.

You could literally have an 8-year-old lining up against a 12 year old—maybe even a 13 year old if they had ever been held back a year. It didn't seem to make much sense. But by my 4th grade year, at 9 years old, I had earned a spot on the starting lineup.

For young Black athletes growing up in Montgomery, there really were no aspirations of playing in the NFL. My 4th grade year was the 1961-62 school year. The NFL was about to be fully integrated, as the last holdout for segregation—the Washington Redskins—caved and got their first-ever Black player for the 1962 season.

But most southern college football teams had not integrated yet. Public elementary and high schools in the south still had not integrated either. So while a handful of Black players might have gotten scholarships from places like USC or Notre Dame, those kinds of dreams weren't on the radar for most of us in Montgomery.

Our biggest aspiration was to play on the local high school football team. The Booker T. Washington Yellow Jackets were some bad boys. The Alabama High School Football Historical Society reports that the Yellow Jackets had an overall winning percentage of 71% across their 28-year history.[1]

At the time we were playing on the elementary school team, the Yellow Jackets were enjoying their longest ever win streak. They won 19 games in a row from September 1962 through September 1964.[2] And they weren't just winning by a little bit. They were making their opponents regret showing up. Just to give you an idea of how good they were, here are the results from the Yellow Jackets 1963 season, courtesy of AHSFHS.org:

1963 Season				
Date	**Opponent**	**Score**		
Wed., Sep. 11	vs. St. Jude	34	0	W
Tue., Sep. 17	@ Laurel	31	6	W
Mon., Sep. 23	vs. Carter Parramore Quincy FL	16	6	W
Fri., Oct. 4	@ Druid	15	6	W
Wed., Oct. 9	vs. Hayes	43	0	W
Wed., Oct. 16	vs. Parker	15	6	W
Wed., Oct. 23	@ Carver Dothan	52	0	W
Fri., Nov. 1	vs. Carver Gadsden	14	0	W
Fri., Nov. 8	vs. Mobile County Training	6	0	W
Sat., Nov. 16	Carver Montgomery	20	6	W	Cramton Bowl

1963 Football Season Booker T. Washington Yellow Jackets

19

Scoring 52 points in a high school football game is no small feat now, and it definitely wasn't back then. This was before the days of spread offenses, run-shoot, fun and gun, no huddle, and all the rest. Besides that, there are only 48 minutes of playing time in a high school game. Also, there were 5 shutouts and the Yellow Jackets allowed no more than 6 points to any opponent all year—when I say they were bad boys, I mean they were bad.

And they were heroes to all the local boys who had any interest in sports, especially Theron and me. Playing for Booker T. was the most substantial sports aspiration I could imagine at that time. It was the biggest dream of my life as a young boy, but even that dream looked to be a bit of a challenge.

NO MORE FOOTBALL

My athletic success was not any kind of problem in regard to achieving my dream of playing for the Yellow Jackets. I had done very well on the elementary school team. But in Montgomery, at that time, there was no such thing as a junior high football team for the Black schools. So after 6th grade your football career was over, at least for a time.

Waiting three years may not sound like a big deal, but to a young boy who wants to play football more than he wants to eat, it was a very big deal. But that was life. There was nothing to do but wait. So Theron and I both waited patiently for football to come back into our lives after we moved beyond elementary school.

Basketball was a poor substitute in my mind. Still, it would have been better than nothing. Unfortunately, I just wasn't as blessed in that sport as I had been in football.

Trying out for the basketball team in 7th and 8th grade, I failed to make the team both times.

So there was no organized sports for me during those years. Then out of nowhere came a huge, unexpected blessing. We got the news that for our 9th grade year, the city of Montgomery would be starting up junior high football teams for all of the Black schools. There had already been junior high football in the white schools, so I suppose maybe it was an equality issue.

Public schools in Alabama did not even begin integration until 1963. This would have been 1966—those were the days when some in Alabama may still have been clinging to the "separate but equal" doctrine. Maybe somebody was scrambling to make things "equal" in the hopes that they could stay separate—I honestly don't know. All I know for sure is that we were going to have football, and I was thrilled beyond measure.

There's no way for me to exaggerate what a blessing this was in my life. For two long years, I had been yearning to play football. As far as I knew there would be one more year to wait, but now I was going to be back on a real football team.

When it came time to put together the team, Coach James Jackson held a meeting and told everyone who wanted to play that they could come and try out. Naturally, every young football player is keen to tell the coaches what position they want to play. But before any of us could even get started down that road, Coach Jackson let us know that the coaches would tell everyone which position would be the best fit for them.

I had been a star running back on the elementary school

team. So everyone knew I played running back—everyone except the new coaches, I guess.

Actually, everyone knew that I *was a* running back. It wasn't just something I played. Running the ball, running over defenders, hurdling past them, getting into the endzone —this was a major part of my identity. So you can imagine my surprise, and my frustration, when the coaches decided to line me up at center.

Forget running back—at that point I would have been thrilled to line up as a wide receiver. Maybe even a tight end. Anything but center!

I couldn't believe it. Doing my best to lobby for a different position, I let the coaches know any way I could that center was not the position for me.

The next thing I know, the coaches were trying me at quarterback! Talk about going from one extreme to the other. They took me from a low "skill" position to the highest skill position on the field. In spite of the fact that I could not throw a football very well, this move stuck. Throughout that season, I played quarterback for my junior high team.

The solution to me not being able to throw was for us to run option most of the time. The coaches didn't have much desire or intent to throw the ball, so they basically put me at quarterback with the plan for me to just run the ball.

It's safe to say that our junior high team far exceeded anyone's expectations. We had some truly great players. Mike Washington—a future NFL great who logged 28 interceptions over 9 seasons with Tampa Bay—was on the team. Mike and I had played against each other in elementary school, and we knew each other from that experience. So we had already been friends and now we were teammates. Mike and I would go on to play at Alabama together a few years later.

But for now, we were all learning to play together and it was a lot of fun. We worked hard and developed into a truly excellent team. There were some other great players on that team. Scott Gholston really stands out in my mind as one of the top athletes I played with across my entire football career (right up there with Alabama teammates Ozzie Newsome and Richard Todd). Scott ended up playing college football at Troy State. Whenever we really needed to throw the ball, they would put Scott in at quarterback and I would line up as a wide receiver.

There were several other really good players, but the entire team deserves credit for a lot of hard work and for coming together and playing well as a group.

At the end of the season, we had won every game we played, including the city championship. God blessed me to be voted MVP of the league. I was also named MVP of the championship game that year after scoring the winning touchdown. We had to throw to win it, so that meant Scott had to come in and throw the winning touchdown to me.

One neat development that season was that the local high school coaches had started to come to our games. They were keen to scout the upcoming talent. What was really interesting was that coaches from some of the local *white* high schools began coming to our games. That was somewhat unexpected because the white high schools in Montgomery had not integrated.

At one point during the season, some coaches from the white high schools approached me and my coach about me possibly coming to their school. One of those coaches was from Robert E. Lee High School in Montgomery. Imagine that. Here I was ready to move on to the next step and fulfill my childhood dream of playing for the Booker T. Washington Yellow Jackets, and now a white coach was asking me to come play for Robert E. Lee!

Saying no really wasn't a matter of Black and white for me. I said no simply because my childhood dream was to be a Yellow Jacket. I wasn't thinking about making history. Bringing about social change wasn't on my mind. I just wanted to be a Yellow Jacket. I wanted to wear that blue and gold uniform and be just like those guys I had idolized all those years before.

As divine providence would have it, I didn't have the final say on playing for Robert E. Lee.

But the decision to say no did affect the next couple of years of my life. Booker T. Washington's coach had been recruiting me as well, and I was very happy to start high school there the next year. Theron was already at Booker T. and already on the football team, playing as a fullback. There was really never any chance of me going anywhere else—at least not willingly.

That 9th grade year was a big stepping stone for me as a football player. I was now known around the city of Montgomery for my skills on the football field. Winning the championship that year and being an important part of that team gave me a lot of confidence—confidence that I really needed after having taken a 2-year hiatus from football.

BOOKER T. WASHINGTON HIGH SCHOOL FOOTBALL

Tenth grade had finally arrived and my lifelong dream was about to be fulfilled. It was time to try out for the Booker T. Washington Yellow Jackets football team and I was pumped.

I'll never forget the first time I stepped out onto the field for tryouts. My reputation had proceeded me. It's not that I was some kind of superstar, but when you are named the MVP of the city, people know who you are. As I walked out onto the field, two big, mean, tough veteran high school players let me know real quick that I was not in junior high anymore.

"You played real good against those little kids, but you're playing with the big boys now. You're not gonna do all that stuff you did back there. You're just a rookie on this team."

They were letting me know my place. That's just the kind of thing kids did to each other back then. The last thing they wanted was for some tenth grader to come in there with a big ego. But truthfully, their comments just made me want to prove myself that much more. It was clear that I wasn't going to waltz onto the Yellow Jackets starting lineup, ushered in by accolades from the previous year. I was going to have to earn my spot.

Willie Scott was a new teammate of mine that year. He was coming from a similar background in that he was a running back who had performed very well at the junior high level during the previous year. Willie had not been on the same junior high team as me, but had played instead on the Booker T. Washington Junior High team in Montgomery. We had played against each other, and we both knew who the other one was before becoming teammates.

Willie and I became instant friends that year, and we bonded due to facing the same obstacle: a bunch of older, tough football players who didn't respect us yet, and were determined to not let anything come easy for us.

Willie and I were not deterred.

The first game that year was against Parker High School out of Birmingham. It was 1968, and Parker was not a bad team at all. Willie ran for over 100 yards and scored a touchdown. I was blessed to score two touchdowns in the game, and we went on to win 32-7. The little rookies ended up leading the team into victory, and it's safe to say we had their respect after that.

Playing at Booker T. was a great blessing. Some of our games were played at the Cramton Bowl, which was a very large and prestigious venue for some high school kids. It was used for minor league baseball games, major league spring training, and the Alabama State College football games.

The stadium capacity was 24,000, and it was actually the first site of a football game in the south to be played at night under electric lights.[3] When I was a young kid, there was nothing like the thrill of seeing the Yellow Jackets emerge victorious from a hard-fought battle.

Booker T. Washington High School was three blocks from the stadium. So after the games, the football players would walk through the neighborhood back to the high school. All of the neighborhood kids, including Theron and me, would be running beside them, scrambling around them. Later on, you could brag that you got to walk next to one of the local heroes. It was magical.

Now we were playing there, and little kids were running around us after a big victory. Scoring frequent touchdowns put a lot of the attention on me. "Ralph! Ralph! You played great tonight, Ralph!" While this was a dream come true and a huge blessing, I also found that it was difficult to keep my ego in check.

During our 10th grade year, quite a few other players from our junior high team were able to contribute as well. Some of the players who had come into the 10th grade from other local junior high schools were also able to contribute. It's a big deal for 10th graders to be able to contribute to a high school team because most of your starters are typically in the 11th and 12th grades. We just had a lot of exceptional talent in our particular class.

That year we started off our season 5-0. Then we had two close losses down the stretch before ending our season with two strong victories. The first was over George Washington Carver Montgomery—our biggest rival—who we beat 24-19. The next week, we beat George Washington Carver Birmingham 26-0 to finish out our season. Overall, it was a great year, and our final record was 7-2.

My 11th grade year, football season started off with a bang. My brother Theron made starting fullback that year, so we both got to start in the backfield together. I'll never forget my dad in the stands at that first game. He was up there like the big man on campus, smoking his big cigars and telling everyone those were his boys in the backfield. Fortunately, we made him proud by both scoring touchdowns in the game.

It made me really happy that we could honor him by doing well that night.

This was the 1969 season. One major development for integration that year was that there would be a single playoff system and state championship game for both Black and

27

white high schools. Previously, the white high schools had their own playoff system and championship game, and the Black schools were not allowed to participate. So this was a major step forward.

Our Booker T. Washington Yellow Jackets were fierce contenders that year under head coach Arthur "Buddy" Davis. Within the local community, there was a lot of hope and excitement that a Black high school might win the first-ever integrated state championship.

We played almost perfect that year, with a 9-0 record in the regular season. Our defense delivered 3 shutouts and held every single opponent to 8 points or less. Our offense always scored plenty of points to win the game, and our closest margin of victory that year was 7 points.

But something unexpected happened in the first round of the playoffs. We got absolutely whipped at Legion Field by Berry High School, one of the largest white high schools in Alabama. Berry is now known as Hoover High School, and they have a legendary football program there. A few years ago, their football program was even the subject of a very popular reality show called *Two-A-Days: Hoover High*.

Berry was really, really good that year. But there was one team that was even better. Berry lost the championship game to Robert E. Lee High School, 14-7. The biggest, most well-known, white high school from Montgomery had won the state championship during the first year of integration.

While BTW had some notable seniors that year, a lot of our starting lineup were juniors. So we had a lot of hope—and a lot of resolve—that our Black high school would take the state championship in 1970. In fact, that became our overriding motivation during the offseason. Taking the state championship for the Black community was going to be a source of pride and accomplishment for us.

If you'll indulge me, I'd like to honor all of my teammates from Booker T. Washington, including a few of them by name: Mike Washington, George Pugh, David Lewis, Willie Scott, Allen Garner, Freddie Pruitt, Frank Pollock, Larry Bowen, Sammy Rose, Willie Mott Bailey, Scott Gholston, Earl Wilson, Harrison Jenkins, Lonnie Broadnax, Donald Calvin, Jackie Tutt, Curtis Smith, Wille Wheat, and Willie Frank Bailey.

This was a very special group of young men. Many of us had been playing together since elementary and junior high. More than 60% of our starters would go on to play at the college level, and some would go onto the NFL. Our team was extremely talented. We just knew next year's championship was ours for the taking.

A DARK DAY

Unfortunately, winning the championship for an all-Black high school was not meant to be. In the spring of 1970, the football players were called in for our first meeting to talk about starting spring practice—or so we thought. All we knew is that we were told, "Anyone who plans to try out for the football team, be at the gym on Friday afternoon at 3 pm."

Everyone who had played the previous year was excited about the meeting. This was our year. Anticipation was incredibly high. The atmosphere at school that week was electric. We just knew from the time of this first meeting that we were going to have something really special this year.

Imagine our surprise when we walk into the gym that day

for a football meeting, and we see three white men in suits and ties—white men that we had never seen before. Now, that may not sound out of the ordinary to some readers. But for our all-Black high school in Montgomery, Alabama, in 1970, this was very out of the ordinary.

Immediately, the sense among the players was that something must be terribly wrong. White men in suits don't come to your football meeting for any *good* reason.

Immediately, we were told, "We have some good news, and some bad news."

Okay, yep. Here it comes. We don't know what hammer they're about to drop. Maybe they are doing away with the integrated playoff system. Or worse, maybe they are cutting funding. What if there are no sports next year at all?

But the news that came was worse than that.

We weren't even going to have a school anymore!

"Booker T. Washington High School will be closing its doors forever at the end of this year. That's the bad news."

No kidding! This high school and its football team were a dream come true for all of us, and a major source of pride and inspiration for our community. *What are they thinking, shutting us down?*

The man who did most of the talking went on to explain, "The good news is that each of you will have an opportunity to try out for the football team at your new schools starting Monday afternoon."

What? Schools? Did he just say 'schools'? That means we're not all going to the same school . . .

The next words out this man's mouth confirmed our worst fears. "Some of you are going to be going to Robert E. Lee High School, some will be zoned for Jefferson Davis

High School, some will be zoned to Sidney Lanier, and some will be zoned to George Washington Carver."

They were splitting us up. Not only were we not going to get to play together, some of us were going to have to go play at the white schools!

I was one of twelve football players who had been zoned for Robert E. Lee High School. While I had heard of the school, I had never even been there that I could recall. I didn't know where the school was or anything about it, but all of a sudden I was going to be playing there.

They announced that some of my best friends and teammates would be zoned for other schools. It was by far the most deflating and disappointing experience of my young life up to that point. That day felt like the darkest day of my life.

But in reality, that day was part of God's plan to shape the direction of the rest of my life.

2

THE CALL OF INTEGRATION

I n life, when you find yourself in a difficult situation, you have to consider what part of that situation is under your control and what part isn't under your control. The opportunity to be the first Black team to win an integrated state championship was gone, and it wasn't coming back. I had no say in that.

I did not have any say in being removed from my beloved Booker T. Washington High School to attend Robert E. Lee High School—a historically and predominantly white high school, which was named after a Confederate general and located in the middle of the deep south. No one asked me if I wanted to be one of the first Black players at this school. They did not come and ask me if I wanted to be a pioneer for the cause of integration.

I was simply thrust into all of this at a moment's notice.

I knew that I could not ultimately control how the people at Robert E. Lee would view me. There was no way for me to control the opportunities they would give me. How they would treat me and speak to me and interact with me was beyond my power to control.

The only thing I really could control was how I responded to the situation. I could control my own behavior. I could respond with class, dignity, and a good attitude. I could go in there and do my absolute best.

I had grown up reading about and watching Malcolm X and Dr. Martin Luther King Jr. on TV. We were very aware of the fight for civil rights that was going on in America, so even at the young age of 17, I realized that God was presenting me with an important opportunity. He was giving me the opportunity to demonstrate that racism was wrong—not by proclaiming and preaching that it was wrong—but by proving that it was wrong through my conduct, my character, and my accomplishments.

That moment of my life caused me to seriously reflect on the challenges and the opportunities ahead. I realized that God was leading me to advance the cause of integration, and that has been a running theme of my life ever since.

FROM BOOKER T. TO ROBERT E. LEE

Monday afternoon came, and our group of twelve walked over to Robert E. Lee High School for the first time. We were going there to become some of the first Black football players at this historically white school.[1]

There was a few miles of distance between the two schools, and getting there meant walking through some of the white neighborhoods which surrounded the school. I will never forget that day.

"We don't want you over here!"

"Go back to your school, [n-word]!"

"We don't need you over here! Best be going back to your own neighborhood!"

It had been in the newspaper the previous weekend that the schools would be integrating and holding tryouts for football, so they knew we would be coming that day. There'd be a few people standing around here or there as we walked through these white neighborhoods. A car would pass here and there, and someone would yell at us from the car.

The truth is that I don't remember feeling scared or threatened or sad. Really, all I remember thinking was, "We must be getting close to the right place, because they're starting to yell at us."

We had never been to the school before and weren't completely sure of how to find it. But after some searching, we did finally make it to the school that day, safe and sound.

FIRST TEAM MEETING

When the coaches walked into that first meeting, they did not like what they saw. The bleachers in the auditorium had three big sections. On the far-left section were seated twelve Black football players. The right section contained every other football player, about 60 or so, all of them white. The middle section was completely empty.

I encountered Coach Jim Chafin for the first time that day. Fortunately for all of us, Coach Chafin turned out to be an amazing coach and a wonderful human being. With Chafin as head coach, Robert E. Lee had won the state championship in football the prior season, which was the 1969 season.

As an assistant under the previous coach, Chafin had won five state championships in eleven years. Before that, he had won the state baseball championship in his first and only year as a baseball coach. So Chafin's coaching credentials were already very well established.[2]

Assistant Coach Pete Lee was in attendance, and Coach James Shannon, a Black coach from Booker T. Washington, was also at the meeting. He had been a basketball coach at Booker T., but he was now going to be an assistant football coach at Robert E. Lee.

Coach Chafin later told us that when they first walked into the room, he spoke quietly to the other coaches and said, "Until we fill in that middle section, we have no hope for a football team."

Many people probably recall the movie *Remember the Titans*, which is the biographical story of a football team in Virginia that integrated in 1971. While many of the real life players from that team dispute much of the racial tensions and other details of that movie,[3] I can tell you that what we experienced at Robert E. Lee High in 1970 was very much like that movie.

Black players and white players were put onto a team together. Barriers were broken. We learned to respect one another. We learned to work together, and to have each other's back.

There were power struggles, with both Black and white players trying to step up as leaders. At the Black schools, we had been constantly told by coaches, older players, and others in the community, things like this: "The white schools don't want to integrate with you guys because you are so much more athletic than they are. They know they can't hang with us on the football field. Those schools like Robert E. Lee win championships—*against other white players*. They know that Black players are better than they are, and they know we would beat the crap out of them. They're really soft, and they just can't play football like we can."

After we got to know some of the white players and everyone began to open up with each other, we learned that they had always been told things like: "Those Black guys may be big, strong, and fast, but they are not smart. We'll beat them every time because they don't understand formations, structures, and systems. If they tried to play with us, they'd be lost and confused. We would win all day, every day."

We had all brought these biases to the table. I fully admit that I went in thinking, "These guys can't play. They're soft."

In the same way, their biases were pretty obvious. It was insulting the way they spoke to me initially. They started breaking down what a 24 dive was for me as though I had never played football in my life. I said, "I know what a 24 dive is. Just give me the ball." They could see pretty quickly that we all knew and understood the game of football very well, so some of the biases were getting challenged right out of the gate.

But because initial practices were not in full pads, the Black guys were the first ones to defy the stereotypes. As the saying goes, "Everybody looks like an All-American in shorts." Until we dressed out in full pads, we were still very much carrying our bias that the white boys "couldn't play."

The first day in pads fully relieved us of our incorrect biases about white players. Really, all it took was one player to do that—a young white guy named Eddie Foster.

Eddie was an All-City, All-County defensive end. He was all of 5 feet 8 inches, and 175 lbs, but for some reason all of the white players acted like they were scared of him. This guy was supposed to be one of their better players? He didn't look intimidating, that's for sure.

But these other white guys on the team were just so afraid of Eddie Foster. We thought, surely this first day of full pads was going to be comical. If the other players on this team are scared to line up against Eddie Foster, we're going to have a field day with them!

We were sure that Eddie Foster *could not have even made our team* at Booker T. Washington. We just didn't get it.

Finally, the first day of pads, we got to see ol' Eddie in action. He lined up against white player after white player, and just manhandled them. He could get past all of them. He could knock them to the ground, or throw them around like they were nothing. Nobody could stop Eddie.

We were more convinced than ever that this was a problem exclusive to white players. We still did not believe that Eddie could handle lining up against a Black player. To prove our point in the most dramatic fashion possible, we picked out the biggest, strongest, beast of a man we could pick. I'm not going to mention his name because he was a great player, and I don't want to mention anyone's name in a negative context.

But this guy was big. Huge. And strong. And athletic. We just knew he was about to teach Eddie—and by extension all of these white players—some lessons they would never forget.

Eddie Foster beat this man one on one in such a dramatic, dare I say, embarrassing fashion, that we basically had to tuck our tail between our legs and backtrack all of our smack talk about white players. We concluded that day that in addition to having some kind of superhuman strength, Eddie Foster was also the meanest human being alive. He showed no mercy on the football field, and he proved to us that yes, white boys can play.

In an ironic twist, those false and negative stereotypes we'd been brought up with might have been the best thing to happen to this team, because we could all see pretty quickly that none of it was true. Those white guys could hit. They could run. They could throw. They were very physical.

And us Black guys could study film, dissect opponents, and break down the X's and O's with the best of them.

I'll never forget the conversation I had with George Pugh as we walked home after the second practice in full pads. George was another Black player who had come over from Booker T. Washington with me. George would go on to be my teammate at Alabama, so we were both pretty good football players.

We were walking home after practice, tired and sore. I looked over at George and just said calmly, "You know, all that stuff the coaches always told us about how those white boys couldn't play . . . I think they lied to us!" By that point, everyone was in agreement—we had gotten some *bad* information.

While I have my suspicions, I wonder what the conversation was like for the white boys that day. All I know for sure is that we all quickly came to respect each other. Stereotypes weren't just broken. They were shattered. Destroyed. Eradicated—on both sides.

And we all grew closer and more unified as a team throughout the season.

COMING TOGETHER

Just like in *Remember the Titans* when the players had to run in the middle of the night through a graveyard, we had our moment where we had to pull together. During late summer, we went through a string of brutal practices that made us feel like we were all going to die. The heat was intense, and the coaches worked us over. It was like they were determined to make sure anyone who was weak wouldn't come back.

But truthfully, the adversity and difficulty of those practices caused us to come together as a team. Toward the end of a particularly long practice in scorching heat, they told us we had to scrimmage 1st team offense against 1st team defense.

As the scrimmage dragged on and guys were dropping from exhaustion, they would tell the offense, "Okay, if you guys score one more time, we'll all get out of here." Then they would give me the ball, and I would score on a long touchdown run.

The coaches would come back and say, "No, that was too easy . . . We're gonna do it again."

Meanwhile, they had been telling the defense, "If you stop these guys one more time, we can all go home." I remember getting tackled one time and I literally could not get up. It wasn't that I was injured. It was that my whole body was done. Finished. I couldn't move.

Some other players picked me up and dragged me back to the huddle. Having just enough time to get some oxygen and regroup physically, I heard the coach say, "Okay, I mean it this time. If you all can score one more touchdown, we're outta here."

I know our offensive line was tired. These were big guys and we'd been going hard all day. Lee Gross, Lamar Langley, and the rest of the offensive line could barely stand up. One of them looked at me and said, "Ralph, if you'll run behind me, I'll make a hole."

They were determined to do their jobs, even when they were hurting and barely able to stand. They earned my respect that day. They also earned the respect of our defense that day. And really, everyone on the team was showing that same fortitude.

Even if there was someone you really still didn't get along with, it was almost like that day, we were all thinking things like, "Man, even if I don't like that guy, I respect him."

Maybe it was pure luck, or maybe it was a rather genius way of getting us to all band together. Either way, it worked. We grew to respect each other greatly, and we came out of that week stronger and more unified than ever. The dividing line of who was willing to make sacrifices and lay themselves on the line had nothing to do with color. It had to do with character and work ethic, and we could all see that plainly now.

The middle section of those bleachers had been filled in, and there was no longer anything that could stop us.

A HISTORY MAKING SEASON

I would love to tell you that our new understanding toward each other as human beings was enough to win football games, but it would not be true. Those things were necessary components of success, but they did not guarantee success.

We still had to work very hard, and we still had to learn to gel together. We had to learn how to work together as a unit—singularly focused on winning.

Our opening game was against Ramsay High. One of the players who had come over with us from Booker T. Washington was named David Lewis. David was one of my best friends. He was a little scatback type of runner—very quick and agile, good at eluding defenders. In that opening game against Ramsay, David returned a kickoff 90 or so yards for a touchdown.

Mike Washington had an interception, and I was blessed to be able to score two touchdowns. So immediately, the new Black players from Booker T. Washington were having a major impact. We won that game 26-14, a result which turned out to be our closest game of the season.

Once we found our groove as a team, there was no stopping us. We destroyed opponents, outscoring them on average 29.4 to 6.8 over our 13 game season. And as it turned out, playing at Robert E. Lee was just as fun and prestigious as Booker T. Washington. We got to play several of our games in the Cramton Bowl that year in front of 24,000 people.

Even though Robert E. Lee now had 12 Black players, the vast majority of the fan base was still white. Over the course of that year, we got to see the attitudes of the fan base change drastically. It started out with that long walk over to the school when the attitude was, "We don't want you here and don't need you here."

Then it went to, "Okay, these guys can contribute to *our* team."

At some point during the season their attitude became, "These are *our* players." They began to view us just like any other player on the team. Color was no longer an issue—they were just happy we were part of the team!

Row one: Paul Bailey, Steve Murphy, Andy Herring, Louis Kral, Jay Thompson, David Lewis, Wes Neymour, Eddie Foster; Row two: Mike Washington, Olen Crawford, Ronnie Davis, Mike Moore, Stan Pau, Johnny Whitaker, William Marshall, Ken Thompson; Row three: Coach Chafin, Robert Brophy, Ralph Stokes, Scott Wigington, Tim Sherman, Lee Gross, Lamar Langley, Keith Wideman, Earl Wilson

The Robert E. Lee High School Football Team 1970 Seniors

About midway through the season, we faced a huge challenge in playing against the Tuscaloosa Black Bears. They had a first team high school All-American middle linebacker who tackled everything that moved. There was no getting past this guy. You might have heard of him—a guy named Sylvester Croom.

In case you haven't, Sylvester went on to become an All-American at Alabama. He also played for the New Orleans Saints before starting a long coaching career that culminated with him becoming the first-ever African American head coach in the SEC.

When we watched him on film, we could see that no one was able to block him. Period. Sylvester was 6 feet and 220 pounds at that time. He was an absolute beast of a man with almost superhuman strength.

The first quarter was an intense battle, with both sides trying to establish dominance. Secdrick McIntyre was my running mate that year in the backfield. Secdrick went on to play for Auburn, and later for the Atlanta Falcons.

Even though Secdrick was a great athlete and a great blocker, he was only in the 10th grade that year. He couldn't have been more than 170 pounds. Early in the game, I was running behind Secdrick as my lead blocker, and he somehow completely missed his block against Sylvester Croom. So I had this freight train of a man running at me full speed.

It was one of the hardest hits I had ever taken in my life. He almost knocked me into the next county. My helmet was turned sideways. I had a huge bruise on my chin. It took me a second or two to get up, and as we walked back to the huddle, I looked at Secdrick and said, "Secdrick, that boy about killed me! Are you going to block him this time? You have to at least get in front of him!"

The game was still very close at that point, and I was feeling like Croom could have easily taken me out of the game if he was left unimpeded again. Fast forward to the next series, and we run that same play. I've got the ball, running behind Secdrick, and I could see this collision coming. It was almost like I was standing outside of the scene, watching it in slow motion. Secdrick definitely wasn't going to miss him this time.

Boom!

I almost stopped in awe of the sound I had just heard. These two men hit each other hard, and the vibration rang out through the stadium like a thunder clap. It was like there was a shockwave from this hit, and both men stood each other straight up for a moment.

Sylvester was a tremendous player, and I give him full credit for that. But Secdrick had found a way to slow him down long enough for me to run past him, and we kept that up for the rest of the game the best we could. That allowed me the opportunity to run four touchdowns, and our team to walk away with a 27-0 victory.

Later on, Sylvester and some of the other players on that team remarked, "We contained every other player on yall's team that night. If we could have contained you, we could have beat you guys." I will never forget that hit between Secdrick and Sylvester. It was like two bulls having a head on collision at full speed.

The headline the next day said something like, "Lee Rides, Stokes Strides." So by that point, my status as a local hero was completely solidified.

The very next week, we played against Dothan High School. We had seen film of Dothan, and they had a defensive lineman that no one could block. His name was Gus White, and he would later go on to be a stud teammate of mine at Alabama. Gus was truly unstoppable. He took 90% of our team's focus going into the game.

The big question on everyone's mind was, "How will we ever get past this guy to score?"

We were very fortunate to have some great offensive linemen in Lee Gross, Lamar Langley, and Ronnie Davis. Lee especially was a star that year. He went on to play for the Auburn Tigers and later the New Orleans Saints. You might have heard of Lee's son, Gabe Gross, who was quite the athlete and ended up playing 7 seasons of major league baseball. The apple did not fall far from the tree.

Our offensive linemen all did a great job that night, and somehow we came away with a 27-6 victory. Later on, when we were teammates at Alabama, Gus told me, "We felt like we didn't tackle you that whole night. You must have run for 150 yards and 2 or 3 touchdowns. Our coaches kept yelling at us, 'Can somebody please tackle that guy?'"

We had gone in worried that we couldn't stop their star defensive lineman, but during the game, they ended up feeling like they couldn't stop us. That game gave me confidence that we could play with anybody and be successful. Those types of moments also helped solidify the unity of our team and our fanbase.

Even after our fanbase began to fully accept us Black players, there were still other challenges. For example, late in the season, we had to travel to Meridian, Mississippi, to play Meridian High School. I can tell you that none of the Black players on the team were excited about that.

The game itself was a big deal—they were the defending state champions for Mississippi. But besides the football challenges, there was another major issue. Most of us Black players had never been to Mississippi before, and everything we had heard about it was not good. Meridian was the exact city where the KKK had murdered three civil rights activists just 6 years prior. Alabama had more than its own share of hate and violence, but we had lived in Alabama and had managed to stay safe. It was familiar.

Going into a new place that is associated with that kind of hate and violence was very daunting. We didn't know how they were going to react to an integrated team. Would they scream at us? Hurt us? Lynch us?

And perhaps the bigger question in our minds was, if they do challenge or threaten us Black players, will our coaches and teammates and fanbase stand up for us? We weren't entirely sure.

When we got there, it was clear that high school football was a big deal in Meridian, Mississippi. They had a huge fan base, and a big, decked out marching band. There was a lot of excitement and enthusiasm for the game. But all of us Black players were still very nervous. We just didn't know what to expect.

All of a sudden, we see that they're rolling out the big paper banner and the football team is lined up behind it. You could basically just see a bunch of cleats at that point. But the moment they broke through that banner, we all breathed a huge sigh of relief.

The first player through the banner was the biggest Black football player I'd ever seen in my life. These were the days when an average high school offensive lineman was 210 pounds, but this guy was easily 300 pounds.

He came running through first by himself, and then the rest of the team followed after him. It gave the impression that he was a major leader on their team, and the whole stadium cheered them on. *Okay, they have a Black player, and they're cheering for him. Maybe Mississippi isn't so bad after all.*

Now that we were past our fears about racial problems, we still had to face off with a very good football team. We had brought 65 players with us. When their team came running through that banner, it seemed like they would never stop coming. Player after player trotted out as though they were being churned from a factory. It turned out that they had dressed 120 players, including their junior varsity team. The whole thing was designed to intimidate us, and it worked.

As we were going through our pre-game warm ups, we couldn't stop thinking about how huge this school must have been. The situation had gone from just the Black players being apprehensive to the whole team being concerned. So again, this was an issue where a common struggle or adversity brought us closer together as a team. There was a strong sense of uniting to overcome this giant we were facing.

In the end, we played really well that night, and won the game 34-18. Three of our defensive backs had interceptions, and that allowed us to really pull away in the game. It was a great night. We got out of Mississippi not only safe and sound, but with a resounding victory. The bus ride back was a huge bonding experience for all of us.

The next week, we faced off with our biggest rival: Sidney Lanier High. This was the other large school in Montgomery that often had a great football team. There were many years of history for that rivalry, and it was known as one of the biggest high school rivalries in the south. As with a few of the other big schools around Montgomery that we played against, Sidney Lanier had some of our former teammates from Booker T. Washington on the team.

Willie Scott, their star running back, had been a longtime friend and a former teammate of mine. Larry Bowen, another friend and former teammate, was also on the team. He told me later that most of their team's strategy discussions that week centered around "how to stop Ralph Stokes."

Larry must have listened because I remember him hitting me really, really hard. But he didn't stop there. When he hit me, he would grind me into the ground and just try to put that extra hurt on me. I didn't know what else to do, so I responded by laughing at him.

That made him mad.

"What are you laughing at, that was a good hit!" Larry was offended.

No way was I going to acknowledge his good hit. "Dude, if that's all you got, you're in trouble," I chided.

Willie Scott, who went on to play college ball at Tuskegee, played a really good game that night. A lot of other guys from Booker T. Washington, including Willie Bailey, also played against us that night and did well. In the end, the Generals were too much for Sidney Lanier. We won the game 28-7.

Me breaking for the sideline as we made our way to the 1970 Alabama State High School Championship

There were several games like that during the season. Our former teammates from Booker T. Washington now played for some of the other local high schools. That meant we were playing against our former teammates. Many of them played well, and I always enjoyed the fact that my former teammates played well. But maybe even more, I enjoyed that our team prevailed every time.

Another notable game that year was against Robert E. Lee

High School of Huntsville. They had a quarterback named Condredge Holloway.

Condredge was a superb athlete who went on to play for the Tennessee Volunteers, becoming the first-ever Black quarterback for an SEC school. Condredge also became a successful businessman, and the Assistant Athletic Director at the University of Tennessee. Given his status as one of the first-ever African American quarterbacks to become nationally prominent, ESPN Films made a documentary film about his life in 2011. It's called *The Color Orange: The Condredge Holloway Story.*

During an amateur interview before the premiere of the film, Condredge was asked, "When you started, did you think about the kind of effect it was going to have on kids and other people?"

His answer imparted some sage advice, "Not at all. I thought about what the defensive end . . . was trying to do to me. Anytime you get your thought process off of football, you will . . . get hurt." Condredge never focused on making history. *But he did make history by focusing on being the best he could be.* He was a great football player. And being a very strong runner in addition to a solid passer, he was very exciting to watch.

So not only was the quarterback excellent, the entire team of Robert E. Lee Huntsville was excellent. They were unbeaten when we faced off against them that year, but our defense put up an absolutely stifling performance, holding their offense scoreless. We won the game, 34-2. There was just no stopping us that year.

I think that win is what caused the Alabama Sports Writers Association to choose me as the state high school player of the year over Condredge. Despite the drastic loss to our team, Condredge still came in second in the voting. He was an absolute superstar on the field, that's for sure. He was also a really nice guy. We got to hang out several times and became friends.

After two easy victories in the playoffs that year, it was finally time to face off against Minor High School in the state championship game. Minor was a tough team. They were undefeated and had already set a school record by winning 12 games that year. They had some great football players.

Tyrone King, who went on to be an All-SEC defensive back at Alabama, was on their team that year. Mike Clisby, who went on to play for Alabama A&M, was also there. In the high school world, these guys were the dynamic duo of wide receivers, scoring touchdown after touchdown throughout the season. We had our biggest challenge of the season against Minor, and we all knew it. Nothing was going to come easy against them.

The first half proved our assessment correct. It was a hard-fought battle, and early in the second half of the game the score was tied 7-7. We had the football coming out of our own end zone. The ball was spotted somewhere between the 0 and 5 yard lines, but I was actually running the ball out of the end zone.

I made it out, and it looked like I would have a decent run. Reaching somewhere around the 10-15 yard line, it felt like we would have a little room to breathe. All of a sudden, one of their linebackers put a mammoth hit on me and jarred the ball loose.

It was very rare for me to fumble, but here I was, after all these years, and all of this work, finally playing in a state championship game. A state championship game in which every yard counted. And I fumbled.

Overcome with emotion, I walked back to the sideline crying. With this being one of those games where both defenses were playing tight—and both offenses were fighting for every inch—it felt like an extremely costly mistake. The despair was overwhelming. I just knew I had cost my team the game.

Mike Washington—the future NFL great that I'd known since 3rd grade and the best friend of my life—walked right up to me, grabbed me, got in my face and yelled, "What are you crying about?"

I babbled out something about fumbling the ball and costing us the game.

"Shut up and stop crying!" As men often do with each other, Mike was speaking forcefully to me as a way to encourage me and get my head right. "I'm going to go get this football back for you. But when I get it back, you better go score a touchdown!"

Mike had just restored hope.

"Go get me the football, and I'll score," I said confidently after gathering myself enough to push out some clear words.

Mike trotted out onto the field with the rest of our defense, and on that very next play, he made good on his promise. Minor's QB dropped back and fired a shot into the end zone, but Mike jumped in front of the receiver and grabbed the ball.

Mike didn't get up celebrating or running around. Instead, he walked all the way over to me, put the football in my chest, and said, "I got you the football. Now you go score."

Some kind of divine providence must have been

happening, because on the very next play, a hole opened up just enough for me to break through the defensive line and go 80 yards for a touchdown. It was a record at that time—longest run ever in a state championship game.

The momentum shift was too much for Minor to overcome. The tight game had been broken wide open. Our lead grew from there, and we won the game 27-7.

It's safe to say we made history that season. When I say that we were just like the *Remember the Titans* movie, I mean it. Our team pulled together throughout the year, overcame adversity, and made history as the first fully integrated football team in Alabama to win a state championship.

In 2017, Duane Rankin wrote an article for *The Montgomery Advertiser* which chronicled some of our history making season.

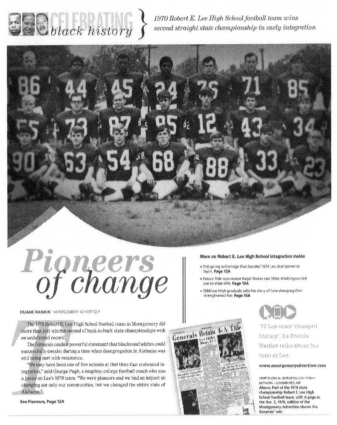

*"Pioneers of Change" Article by Duane Rankin, Montgomery Advertiser,
February 26th, 2017 © Montgomery Advertiser – USA TODAY
NETWORK*

The Black players ended up making huge contributions that year. Mike Washington led the team in interceptions. George Pugh, who would also go on to play at Alabama, was number two on the team for interceptions.

I led the team in rushing, with roughly 2,000 yards and 20 touchdowns. Sedrick McIntyre had something like 15 touchdowns and 1600 yards. David Lewis, another Black running back and kick returner, had his share of touchdowns. All in all, it's safe to say that integration was a huge net positive for Robert E. Lee, and the fanbase knew it. There was no denying it.

In 2019, I was voted into the Lee High School Football Hall of Fame, joining several other African Americans who played on the 1970 team.

When God's hand moved to take me to Robert E. Lee, I began to understand that He had a calling on my life to advance the cause of integration. My role was not to preach. It was not to hold rallies. My assignment was not to get in people's face and tell them how wrong they were.

Instead, the assignment God gave me was to prove racism wrong through my conduct, my character, and my pursuit of excellence. This calling would follow me throughout my life.

Wherever you find yourself in life, the big key is to seek the Lord and then make the most of the opportunity you are given. Things may not turn out the way you wanted, but you can persevere and excel wherever you are.

3

INTEGRATION COSTS SOMETHING

Overall, we had a great experience playing football that year, but there were challenges. Robert E. Lee High School was still very much a white school—with a heritage that wasn't exactly advanced in regard to race relations. Early on, there was name calling, harassment, and use of the n-word at school. It wasn't a friendly, welcoming environment for Black kids to say the least.

Even though things began to turn for the football players at some point during the season—at least in terms of building personal relationships and having broader acceptance—we still felt out of place in a lot of ways.

THE CONFEDERATE FLAG AND DIXIE

If I had to try to think of some things that would make young Black people feel unwelcome, I would say the Confederate flag would be pretty high on the list. But when we got there, a huge Confederate flag still hung in the gymnasium at Robert E. Lee High. So anytime you were in

PE class or in an assembly of some kind, there it was. In your face.

Some people felt that the flag was celebrating their heritage, but what exactly was that heritage? Was it one of love? Peace? Acceptance?

None of us Black kids were happy about the flag. On top of the school name and the flag, the marching band actually used to play the song "Dixie."

My friend George Pugh didn't think that was right. None of us did, but George wasn't going to sit back and do nothing. He actually helped lead a protest by Black students to have the Confederate flag removed.

When given the opportunity to weigh in on the issue, some of us Black football players let our voices be heard. We respected that some people have a different view of the flag, but it definitely wasn't our flag. It did not represent us. And since we were now part of the school, we didn't believe it should be representing our school either.

The administration listened to our concerns, and eventually the flag was removed. "Dixie" was also discontinued from the band's playlist.

BLACK POWER

About midway through our football season, there was another incident that exposed some underlying issues at the school.

During a road game, I broke open a long run and while making my way into the end zone, I raised my arm in celebration. At the end of my arm was a hand. That hand was balled up into a fist, and this was apparently a huge problem for some people.

As I ran to the sideline, I could see that Coach Chafin looked like he'd just seen a ghost. Everyone thought I had just raised my fist to declare "Black power" while running into the end zone.

The ironic thing is, I actually wasn't thinking about that at all. Maybe subconsciously I had that symbol in my mind somewhere. But I can say for sure that when I ran into the end zone, I wasn't trying to make any kind of political statement. I wasn't trying to make any kind of statement at all.

I was just celebrating a touchdown run.

Before that, I had not realized the kind of pressure Coach Chafin must have been under. He had to deal with complaints all day every day for the next week or so about me making a "Black power symbol" in the end zone. People were mad. They were mad at me, and mad at Coach Chafin because he hadn't "disciplined" me for the incident.

It turns out that Coach Chafin had already resisted a lot of prejudice and pressure just to have us out there on the field. He had to fight in order to put his best players in the game, if those players were Black.

Realizing this, and knowing that he was a good coach who treated us as fairly as he could, I did not want to cause any kind of trouble for him or the team. Coach Chafin resisted all of the calls to bench me, and I was more careful about how I celebrated my touchdowns from that point on.

NOT WHAT I SIGNED UP FOR

During the spring semester of my senior year at Robert E. Lee, I had a major wake-up call. Integration would bring challenges even more serious than the ones I had faced during football season.

February is designated as our National Black History Month. At the Black high schools, Black history month was always a *huge* deal. There was basically a month-long celebration, and we never took a year off from recognizing those who had gone before us.

From the time we first came into elementary school—which at that time was 1st grade for most kids—and every year since, we had celebrated Black history during February. But at Robert E. Lee, they didn't have any Black history month celebration.

Robert E. Lee had started integrating, but the school was probably still 90% white. The school was named after a Confederate general, and as I mentioned before, a huge Confederate flag still hung in the gymnasium. Many people at the school were pretty serious about celebrating their southern heritage in those kinds of ways. They had no desire or frame of reference for something like Black history month.

There's no way for me to overemphasize the importance of Black history month. Throughout American and world history, tremendous good and advancement has always been accomplished by Black inventors, writers, soldiers, poets, pastors, scientists, explorers, business leaders, and so on—but their names and accomplishments never made it into the mainstream books and textbooks. The prevailing historical narratives largely ignored the accomplishments of African Americans in the United States.

This kind of approach reinforces a false narrative to young Black people: that they aren't meant to do anything significant. Of course, nothing could be further from the truth. So one of the major goals of Black history month is to inspire confidence in young Black people. You can be a great inventor, like George Washington Carver.

You can be a bestselling author, like Frederick Douglass and Maya Angelou.

You can be an influential world leader, like Nelson Mandela.

You can be a CEO, like Rosalind Brewer.

You can be a business owner. An attorney. An astronaut. A doctor. You can make medical breakthroughs that impact millions of lives.

Young Black people need to know that they can do these things, and that nothing can stop them.

Some of the textbooks back then may have mentioned that George Washington Carver did some work with peanuts, but his accomplishments were likely to be vastly understated. He developed more than 300 agricultural, industrial, and commercial products in his lifetime, and many now consider him to be the father of biochemical engineering. Carver was an advisor to world leaders in his time, and he developed farming methods that still help feed the world to this day.

And while most textbooks back then taught about Amelia Earhart, they did not teach about Bessie Coleman, a highly-skilled Black female pilot who had to go to France to learn how to fly because the flight schools in the US would not accept African Americans. She became one of the best stunt fliers in the country, often using her platform to speak about issues of race before her untimely death in 1926.

Yet many of you reading this book have never heard her name in your entire life.

Inspired by Bessie Coleman's life and accomplishments,

another notable Black aviator, Lieutenant William J. Powell, wrote in 1934, "We have overcome that which was worse than racial barriers. We have overcome the barriers within ourselves and dared to dream."[1]

From Horace King to Jane Bolin to Lewis Latimer to Matthew Henson, there are countless examples like Bessie Coleman hiding in the shadows of history. Shining light on their achievements is what Black history month is all about.

But as February was about to roll around in 1971, the Black students began to realize that there would be no Black history month at Robert E. Lee High School—that is, unless we did something about it. Some of the Black students got together and sought an audience with Principal Carter, the head administrator at the school.

His response was basically, "Nope. We won't be having a Black history month celebration." The only explanation he gave was, "We don't do that at this school. We have history, but we don't have a separate program for Black history."

The Black students' response was, "You don't understand. This is important to us. It's part of our culture. We've always had a Black history month program. We have to have one."

Again, the answer was no.

The Black student community was not about to give up. Somehow, a few of them got the idea to come back to me and say, "Ralph, you were the captain of the football team. Out of all of us, you're the one they respect. You have to go on behalf of the entire Black community and influence them to let us have a Black history month program."

My response was, "Okay, well, I don't know how much influence I really have, but I am certainly willing to try. Black history month is very important. I fully support it, so yes, I'm willing to go fight this fight."

The next day, I had a meeting with Principal Carter and the guidance counselor who was in charge of schoolwide programs. I did my best to make the case for a Black history month program.

There were a couple more meetings, and finally we got this answer, "Yes. You can have a Black history month program. You can have it during school, but it will be voluntary. Any student who wants to attend can attend, but it will not be mandatory."

At that point, I took the news back to the Black Student Council, a student government group that had been spearheading the effort to establish a Black history month program. Thinking I was delivering good news, I was a little perplexed by their response.

This was not good enough.

They basically said, "No. We don't want a *voluntary* program. We have an important speaker coming. He's going to talk about some of the important achievements of Black people. He's part of the NAACP, and it's going to be educational, so this should be mandatory education for everyone."

After some further discussion, everyone seemed to be in agreement. "This is our opportunity to educate the white people on Black achievements. They don't understand these things because it's not taught in their textbooks. So this is our chance to educate the white people *especially*. We have to make this mandatory for everyone, just like every other educational school program. Go back, Ralph, and fight the fight some more."

Somewhat reluctantly, I agreed. It's not that I didn't agree with what they were saying. I did. But I also felt like we had made some serious progress already. I just wasn't sure I wanted to personally go back and ask for more. I had gotten some concessions in my previous negotiations, and we had all walked away on good terms. There was goodwill. Everyone seemed happy with the arrangement.

Now I had to go back under a new premise and ask for more. That was a little uncomfortable.

Nonetheless, I went back and explained once again that this was very important to us. But this time I added that it was our sincere desire to educate *white people* on some of the great achievements of Black people throughout history.

There was some struggle. After a few more discussions, they finally agreed. Yes, we could have our Black history program. And, yes, it would be mandatory for everyone.

The morning finally came. This was our moment. We had fought hard and won, and now it was time to enjoy the fruit of our labors. The mostly white student body, along with most of the faculty, would be hearing a presentation on Black achievements throughout history. What a day.

Only, *that* day never happened.

Something happened, but it was not at all what anyone had described beforehand.

There I was on the front row, excited to hear our guest speaker—a civil rights leader. He came in, and as soon as he opened his mouth, all of my excitement was gone. There was only shock as I listened.

The best I can recall, the first words out of his mouth were, "Oh, my God! This is so exciting! It is such a great day. We are here. The Black people are here at Robert E. Lee High School, and we are taking over! We are dominating!"

What!?!

What in the world was he talking about? Taking over? Dominating? He was supposed to be doing an educational presentation about Black achievements throughout history. I was dumbfounded.

At the same time, I was saddened. I know that he was probably just excited to see Black people making progress. But the way we defeat racism is through proving racism wrong. The way we prove racism wrong is through our conduct and our character.

He continued by asserting that Robert E. Lee was turning over in his grave because the Black people were here and we were taking over. While many of the Black students erupted into cheers, pretty much all of the white students promptly got up and walked out.

Who could blame them?

If someone started talking about white people taking over and dominating, I probably would have walked out.

The rest of his speech, as I recall, was basically a great Black pride rally speech. If we had been at a civil rights rally, I probably would have cheered. It was emotional, and if given in the right venue, it would have been inspiring. There was yelling. There were rally cries. There was cheering.

But I wasn't cheering.

This was not what I had signed up for. There was absolutely nothing educational about the speech. There was nothing unifying about it.

We had a golden opportunity to challenge many wrong biases and prejudices that existed among our peers. Instead, we had probably only caused them to dig in their heels.

Beyond those obvious problems, I had personally stuck my neck out. I had goodwill in the community, and I had leveraged that goodwill to make this event happen. But the people who had set this up did not do what they told me they were going to do. There was no attempt to bring people together. We had a chance to do something positive and healthy to further the cause of integration, understanding, and harmony among the races. Instead, we had done the opposite.

I felt betrayed.

This led to yet another problem. My disappointment and frustration showed. There was no way for me to hide it, and that caused many in the Black community to turn against me.

They thought that what had just happened was wonderful. The way they saw it was basically, "Hey, we just had a great rally and ran these white people out of their own auditorium! That is cool! That is exciting! What is your problem, Ralph?"

Certain that I was in the right, I did not back down at all. "That is not at all what we said we were going to do. That is not the purpose we outlined."

So now all of the white people are upset at me for having brought all of this about. They thought I had lied to them. Besides that, they weren't happy about what had taken place, and I was the primary cause in their minds.

At the same time, many of the Black people were upset at me for not celebrating this Black pride rally they'd just had in the middle of Robert E. Lee High School. They began referring to me as an "Uncle Tom" and a "sellout."

At that point, all kinds of rumors and attacks started swirling around the community.

"He thinks he's too good for the Black people. That's why he went to a white school in the first place."

It got so nasty that I would walk down the hallway at school and it was like the parting of the Red Sea. Nobody wanted to stand near me or talk to me. The only people that would still talk to me or hang around me were a few of my football friends, and my longtime girlfriend.

At that time, there was a local talk radio show led by a guy named Tracy Larkin. Tracy had me on the show a few times during football season. I could not do every interview I was asked to do back then just because we were so busy. But I always liked Tracy and respected him, so I always agreed to his interview requests. I normally listened to his show as well.

One Sunday afternoon, I was sitting at home listening to the radio, and the call-in portion of Tracy's show started. Some of my classmates began calling into the show to tell Tracy what a sellout and Uncle Tom I had become. Once a few of them did it, that opened up the floodgates. Everyone wanted to call in and give their opinion of what a terrible human being I was.

This one girl that I knew as a classmate—I could recognize her voice—called in and said, "I never liked him. I've known him for years, and he's always been arrogant. I'm glad that we can all finally see who he really is."

She went on for quite a while, and it was tough to listen. Now keep in mind that not even two months prior, I had been a local football hero. At the time we were winning the state championship, it sure felt like everyone liked me. If anyone didn't like me, they did a good job of keeping it secret. But now the opposite was true.

What really shocked me that day was when Tracy responded to this classmate who had called in.

"Yeah, I've talked to him several times. He is pretty arrogant. He probably does think he's better than the rest of us."

What?

Where did that come from? There had never been anything but positive conversations and glowing feedback from this man. It just goes to show how a divisive, accusing spirit can spread through a group of people so quickly and without any rational explanation. Surely Tracy knew better than what he was saying. Surely he did not believe the words coming out of his own mouth.

There was no one—not a single person—that called and said, "None of this is true. Ralph is not a bad guy. He's not an Uncle Tom." No one even said, "Hey, let's give Ralph the benefit of the doubt." Instead, it was a free-for-all smear campaign.

Sitting there with my mother and my brother, listening to what felt like my entire city bashing me and attacking everything about my character, I had enough. It was not anger, but rather just a sense that I finally had to defend myself.

I said, "I have to call in and just talk to Tracy. I have to understand why he would do this."

My brother said, "Ralph, you can't do that. They don't want to hear from you."

"I don't care about them. I just want to talk to Tracy. I don't understand why he would do this."

This was a guy that I trusted. That I had respect for. Up until that day, I believed he had respect for me too. For him to sell out on me like that . . . It just didn't make any sense.

Finally, Sandra Sanders, my longtime girlfriend at the time, called in to defend me. She explained that my whole position was that I had been misled. I had gone to bat for something that turned out to be a lie, so I had every reason to be upset.

After she was off the air, I called the radio station myself.

I told the station manager, "I don't want to be on the air. I just want to talk to Tracy off the air."

He said, "Okay, let me see if I can get Tracy for you off the air."

The manager comes back after a few minutes and says, "Okay, I've got Tracy for you."

The next thing I hear is Tracy's voice saying, "Hi folks, this should be interesting. We have with us *live on the air* right now, Ralph Stokes, who's calling to tell us why he was not happy with the Black history program."

I retorted, "You know, Tracy, I didn't want the call to be on the air. I was just calling to talk to y—"

"No, you're live! Right now on the air in Montgomery, Alabama, so let's talk."

"Okay, Tracy, well first let me say that I will answer any questions that you have of me, if you can just give me a minute first to make a statement."

"Okay, go ahead, make your statement."

At that point, I basically told the whole story, explaining my perspective on the way things turned out. I even explained that one of my missions in life was to help the cause of integration, but I felt that we had done the opposite of that.

I explained that I was all for civil rights rallies, and that I respected and fully supported the civil rights leader who had come to the school. However, I did not support what had happened that day, because it was a lie. It's not what we said we were going to do.

I wrapped up my speech, "So if being honest means I am an Uncle Tom, then fine. I'm an Uncle Tom. I just don't believe we should lie to people. I will always stand on my principles, and one principle I live by is that what I tell you

I'm going to do, that's what I will do. If you don't like that, and that's not acceptable to the Black community, then I'm sorry you all feel that way. But I want to stand on the truth of my word. That's all."

He asked a few questions, and there were a few follow up calls.

At that point, some people started to change their tune. A few people were now saying, "I do see his point on that. I respect him for wanting to stand on his word."

Others called in and said, "Nah, he's just making all of that up because he's an Uncle Tom."

The good news is that the radio show represented the beginning of the end of that episode in my life. Before that show, no one could see it any way besides the way they were already seeing it. I was either a liar or an Uncle Tom, depending on whether you were white or Black.

But after the show—slowly but surely—people did start coming back to me. They would say things like, "Hey, I didn't realize where you were coming from. I respect how you stood up for what you believe." Tracy and I enjoyed a very good relationship from that point forward as well.

There were others who apologized. That seemed to forge a stronger bond between us. Going through adversity and misunderstanding—and working to overcome it—has a way of bringing people together. But there were some classmates that never came back to me to reconcile. To this day, we've never had a relationship again. To me, that's kind of sad, but I don't see much I could have done differently. I'm sure I wasn't perfect, but I handled that situation the best way I knew how from start to finish.

Keep in mind, I was a 17-year-old kid who was really content to be focused on cars, sports, and girls. But even at that age, I always tried to take opportunities to make a difference. Opportunities present themselves in life. They can be rare when you're starting out, but if you keep taking them and making the most of them, that will continue opening new doors. In other words, the more opportunity you seize, the more opportunity you will have.

Opportunities to advance equality for Black people is just one type of opportunity. You will have others that matter just as much or more for your personal life than anything else. But if you are a minority, pretty much everything you achieve ends up furthering the cause of equality. And if you ever have an opportunity to *directly* further the cause of equality, I would encourage you to charge forward and do not look back. Remember that to whom much is given, much is required.

The cause of integration was not always easy or fun. It was never cheap. There is always a cost of some kind, and at times, it was very costly. But there's never been any doubt in my mind that it was worth the cost.

Future generations have had it better because of the risks people took and the sacrifices people made in my generation. We had it better because of the daring, bold, and extremely risky undertakings of past generations. And future generations will have it better because of the things you achieve in your life. That's the way it is, and it will always be that way.

Sacrifice begets blessings.

And blessings beget more blessings, as long as they are appreciated.

4

MAJOR INFLUENCES

I grew up as one of five siblings, and I'm the first to admit that we all had some major advantages in life. My oldest brother, Frank Jr., had a 161 IQ—a certified genius. Frank Jr. was basically a stay-at-home dad for most of his adulthood—a noble but unsung profession. He had graduated with a history degree from Alabama State University, but the choice to stay at home with the kids was best for his family.

I always looked up to my brother, and his choice of profession did nothing to diminish his wisdom and value to our family. He raised six kids, who went on to be very successful in many different endeavors. His life was a tremendous success.

My other brother, Theron, was also very intelligent. He went on to become an attorney. Theron is currently the Associate Executive Director for the Alabama Education Association, which is the teachers union for public school teachers in Alabama. He's very successful. My oldest sister, Diana, received a business degree from Tuskegee University with a concentration in accounting. My youngest sister,

Marilyn, became a nurse after graduating with a B.A. in Nursing from the University of Maryland. So we all did well in life.

Someone reading might be thinking, "Well, you all were smart, athletic, and had a good upbringing. I don't have all of those advantages. What can I do?"

Here is the key: We all used what God gave us. God gave some of us exceptional talents. He gave some of us the ability to pursue business. Others law. Others a thriving home life. But my family members who stood out from the crowd all have this one thing in common—they took full advantage of everything God gave them. They made the most of it.

You can be smart and do absolutely nothing. There are extremely intelligent people on this planet who shirk responsibility and end up living in their parents' basement as adults. No amount of talent guarantees success, and there is no lack of talent which cannot be overcome. The key is to figure out why God put you on this planet, and then make the most of the opportunities presented to you.

Another strong advantage we had growing up was the wisdom and strength of my mother. Whereas Dad was the perennial businessman, hard worker, and provider of the family, Mom was the educator, the disciplinarian, and our guiding light. She was very proactive in making sure we stayed on top of our studies, always stressing the value of education to us. Mom was also involved in the community and the PTA. She was just an all-around vigilant and attentive mother.

Perhaps the most important advantage we had was a highly active spiritual life. I cannot stress enough the importance of an active relationship with God, and active involvement in the local church. For a person who wants to achieve everything they are called to achieve in life, those two aspects of life are crucial.

None of us were perfect growing up. Moral perfection is not a requirement because it's not realistic for any of us to achieve that. But no matter what mistakes we make, the key is to stay active in our relationship with God. Don't ever turn your back on Him. And even if you do make that mistake for a time, turn around and come back to Him. He is ready and waiting for you.

Looking back, I am very grateful for the spiritual consistency we experienced growing up. We didn't stay with a single church, or a single denomination, but we never wavered when it came to being involved in church and having God in our lives.

The first church I remember attending was North Montgomery Baptist Church. My dad had been a deacon in his previous church, but that was before I was born. Spiritually speaking, one major thing I remember about my dad was that he knew his Bible.

He could quote verse after verse of the Bible right off the top of his head. It was almost like he had a photographic memory when it came to the Bible. If you were struggling to remember a certain passage, he could tell you where it was and what it said. If you had a question about a specific topic, he could quote you multiple scriptures that addressed the topic.

It was really amazing. As good as his memory may have been, he certainly did not get to that place in life by *not* reading his Bible. He obviously labored and studied over God's Word until he knew it by heart.

My mother was very spiritual, and she attended church every time the doors were open. For many years, even when we didn't want to go, she always made sure her children were in church. Frank Jr. and my oldest sister, Diana, both gladly attended church with my mother.

Theron, myself, and my youngest sister, Marilyn, at some point began attending Newtown Church of Christ, which was right next to our house. My great grandmother, who lived with us, had helped fund the building of this church. That particular church was officially founded by attorney Fred Gray, who was a major civil rights leader.

FRED GRAY

Mr. Gray served as an attorney for both Martin Luther King Jr., and Rosa Parks. He litigated quite a few major civil rights cases, including the case that ruled bus segregation unconstitutional.

Mr. Gray also won NAACP vs. State of Alabama, which ensured the right of the NAACP to operate in the state. They had previously been denied their right to exist and operate in Alabama by the state attorney general.

In the early 60s, Mr. Gray successfully filed suits and led activism that brought about the desegregation of Auburn University, and later on, of all public schools in Alabama that had not already been ordered to integrate.

He was one of the first African Americans elected to the Alabama state house of representatives. He was also the first African American to serve as President of the Alabama State Bar—something that did not happen until 2001. Friends, there are still plenty of "firsts" to be achieved!

Fred Gray has remained active in church and government throughout his life. At the time this is being written, he is still alive and active at the age of 90. In fact, he was serving in the Alabama State House of Representatives until 2015. Today, he is still preaching whenever possible as well as granting interviews from time to time.

In a recent interview with the *Christian Chronicle*, Mr. Gray was asked for his thoughts on injustice. He responded, "I saw injustices being done then, and I thought that somebody needed to be doing something about it. I thought Black people had problems in Montgomery, and I decided I wanted to help solve those problems. I made a commitment as a teenager that I was going to become a lawyer. Less than six months after passing the Alabama bar, I had my first civil rights case, the case of Claudette Colvin, a 15-year-old Black girl who did what Mrs. Parks did, but did it nine months prior."[1]

Fred Gray is a very inspirational figure, and it's easy to see why my great grandmother wanted to help support his church. So it happened for a time that the three youngest siblings, which included me, went to church there with my great grandmother. We went every Sunday and every Wednesday night, and it became our home church for years. It's safe to say that Mr. Gray had significant influence in my life, but like most young people, we still struggled with wanting to go to church.

A SPIRITUAL FOUNDATION

At some point, Theron and I became consumed with our desire to be great athletes. This caused an internal conflict for us. Church often conflicted with being able to watch NFL games on Sunday. I remember that there were several times we really wanted to skip church because of an important NFL game that started at 12 pm central.

Neither my mother nor my great grandmother were receptive to that idea. But as we got older, we continued lobbying to skip church in order to see certain games. Finally, they gave us a choice. They told us that skipping church would be allowed. They were not going to force us to attend church any longer.

They explained that at some point in life, you have to start taking responsibility and making your own decisions. Each person has to make their own decisions regarding their spiritual life, they concluded. They had given us the foundation and it was up to us to build on it.

In a way, this announcement was exciting, but at the same time, we knew it sounded too good to be true. Sure enough, it was. Mother and Grandmother (we called her Grandmother even though she was our great grandmother) went on to explain that if we chose not to go to church on Sunday, that was completely fine. We just couldn't do anything else on Sunday either.

No sports. No TV. No hanging out with friends. No playing outside. But again, we were assured we didn't *have to* go to church. We got the message, and that was the end of our requests to skip church. This was not just a ploy or a manipulation. They truly gave us freedom of choice on attending church, and they were serious about it. They just made sure the alternative was as unappealing as possible.

Looking back, I'm thankful for the spiritual foundation that was laid. Even though it was something I may not have found particularly interesting at the time, there was tremendous spiritual value imparted to us during those years. It's good for a young person to stay in church, even if you sometimes feel like you'd rather be doing something else. The foundation that gets laid down will benefit you all throughout your life.

MOTHER

My mother, Johnnie Mae Stokes, was an interesting person. She loved football, and was a huge Dallas Cowboys fan. Nobody else in our family was a Cowboys fan, at least until my youngest sister, Marilyn, came along and joined my mother. But despite being the lone Cowboys fan in the house for a long time, she was die hard. There were quite a few yelling matches at Thanksgiving over football games that involved the Cowboys. The rest of us just didn't pull for them.

As much as my mother loved watching football, no one could convince her to come and watch her children play. She was alright with us playing . . . She just couldn't watch it happening. Football was a violent game, and she did not want to watch her kids getting hurt. The idea was too much for her.

So she never saw any of my games from elementary or junior high school. Finally, she did get to participate in some way by the time I got to Booker T. Washington. Our games were broadcast on the local radio station, and she would listen to every game and cheer us on. But no one could make her come and watch us.

The truth is that we did get hurt. And the listening might have been worse at times, depending on how the announcer described what was happening. One time she heard the announcer say, "Ralph Stokes is down and he's not moving." Then they went to commercial!

So she sat nervously waiting for any kind of update. If she

had been at the game, she would have seen that I had already walked off the field. Instead, she had to wait until the commercial break was over to hear the announcer say that I had been "gingerly" helped off the field. I had been hit in the ribs, and I knew I was hurt.

But at halftime we went into the locker room and the staff sprayed my side with some kind of liquid ice. Whatever this stuff was, it completely numbed my whole left side. They asked how I felt, and I told them I felt fine. There was no pain at all. So I went back and played in the second half.

I didn't play a lot in the second half but as it turned out, any playing time was too much. The whole game I had felt fine. I even went to bed that night feeling okay. But in the middle of the night, I woke up screaming in severe pain.

I thought I was dying.

My mom and dad rushed me to the hospital. The team doctor met us out there. He explained that my ribs were cracked and that I could have easily punctured a lung. One bone was very close to doing that, and I was in tremendous pain. Just breathing was incredibly painful, and you can't stop breathing, so there was no option except to deal with the pain.

As it turned out, my mother's fears were not unwarranted and I learned to be more careful about dealing with injuries. My mother also softened her stance after I became a full-fledged adult. She did attend some of my games to watch me play at Alabama.

My mother was full of wisdom, and she wanted us to develop wisdom ourselves. I remember when the Selma to Montgomery civil rights march was being planned in 1965. She immediately ruled out the possibility of us younger children going because she did not feel that it would be safe for us.

The older kids, both Diana and Frank Jr., were given the choice to go. My mother didn't pressure them either way. She always wanted us to think, pray, and evaluate our own options in life, and then make our own decisions.

She taught us good values and instructed us thoroughly in life. And of course there was normal discipline. Obedience was expected of us. But when it came to situations like this, she wanted us to experience the personal growth that comes with taking responsibility and making one's own decision. Both Frank Jr. and Diana decided to attend.

The rest of us were home watching on television. We could see the people marching. We could see people protesting the march. If I remember correctly, we could even see Klansmen with their white robes and everything. As we talked about the events of the day, my mother said something to me that I'll never forget:

"Not every Black person that raises their fist and says, 'Black power' is your friend. And not every white person is your enemy. I challenge each of you to judge people, not based on the color of their skin, but by how they treat you and how they treat other people."

For whatever reason, that statement stuck with me. It could have been the significance of the moment or the significance of her words. It was probably a mix of both, but what I know for sure is that her words helped carry me through my time at Robert E. Lee High School and beyond. They made a tremendous difference in my life. The words we speak to our children are very important.

5

THE #3 RUNNING BACK IN AMERICA

As we experienced success during the 1970 football season at Robert E. Lee, the community began to rally around us. Our team started to become the local heroes for the entire city of Montgomery, especially down the stretch when we began to beat our in-city rivals. At that point, it became clear that we were the most serious contenders for the state championship from inside the Montgomery area.

The local press began to sing our praises and enthusiasm continued to grow. Also, recruiting really began to pick up the more attention our team got. Scholarship offers started to pour in and that got individual players a lot of attention.

George Pugh and Secdrick McIntyre were probably being recruited at some level, but they were still underclassmen. Mike Washington, Robert Brophy, Lamar Langley, and Lee Gross were all seniors and being heavily recruited alongside me. My recruitment was described by some at the time as the highest profile recruitment in the history of the state of Alabama. Expectations were extremely high for me at the next level.

I was rated the #1 running back in the South, and the #3 running back in the nation. I was also chosen as a High School All-American.

A HIGH PROFILE RECRUIT

The attention was overwhelming. Sports writers would write stories about me. People would talk about me on TV and radio. And there were scholarship offers pouring in from all over the country.

There was also a good bit of attention on me and the other Black players due to the integration issue. A lot of reporters and commentators wanted to talk about what it was like to be a Black player at Robert E. Lee High School. The good thing was that all of the media attention was from a positive perspective.

In general, the media was not trying to stir racial trouble or bring division. But they did want to talk about what it was like to be in that position, the challenges that had to be overcome, and other topics along that line. The truth is that sports really made integration at the school a lot easier for people.

There were still integration problems when it came to academics—situations where people felt like they were being treated differently because they were Black. Some of the leading Black students in academics at Booker T. Washington had come over to Robert E. Lee. Many of them felt that their abilities were not being respected.

All in all, things weren't going nearly as well for Black students in the areas outside of sports. So there was still plenty of good land to be taken, and people had to fight for every inch of progress in those areas. We had to fight for equality on the football field too, but we had much quicker success. Maybe athletic ability is harder to deny. It's probably also that people's desire to win caused them to accept us much more quickly. This brought unity to a place where division might have otherwise lingered.

Sports, and especially football, caused Black and white people to find common ground. We had the same goals, and we unified to fight against the same opponents each week. We weren't just some guys at school—we were teammates. And the community which gets built around a winning football team is a powerful force.

Again, all of this was very positive for me in the sense that people were excited and enthusiastic about what was happening. We weren't being criticized or harassed—it was quite the opposite. But still, the attention and fame were a lot for a 17-year-old boy to handle. There was a lot of hype around me and at some point, I began to believe it.

There was a struggle for me to just stay grounded. When everyone is constantly telling you how great you are, you begin to believe that message. I had started to think I was the best thing since night baseball.

By late in the season, I had football scholarship offers from Notre Dame, USC, Georgia, Auburn, Tennessee, Alabama, Oklahoma, and many others. Basically, you name a big-time football program and they had offered me a scholarship. I had more than 100 written scholarship offers.

Some of those offers had come from historically Black colleges like Tuskegee Institute, Alabama State College, Grambling, and Jackson State. A lot of people tried to sell me on the idea that I should make a decision to keep Black talent at the Black schools. I'm not saying I never considered it, but it seemed like a strange argument given that African

Americans were fighting fiercely for integration at that time.

Maybe some Black players were called to do that, and maybe others weren't. As I mentioned previously, I continued to feel that God had a call on my life for the cause of integration. It wasn't that I always planned it out, but it sure seems like He did.

One thing I can say about the recruiting process is that I felt a lot of pressure from all sides. It felt like everyone wanted something from me, and they all appeared to be acting out of self-interest. It was very difficult to find anyone that seemed like they were actually concerned about what would be good for Ralph Stokes.

Sandra was still my girlfriend at that time. We had been dating for a couple of years, and that made people feel like she had a lot of influence on my decision. So people went after her, with a few schools actually offering her a scholarship *if* she could persuade me to come along with her. There was a lot of pressure and stress, and it really got out of hand.

At one point, the governor of Alabama even called me on the phone and said, "Ralph, I just wanted you to know that you're very talented, and I think it would be really nice if you took your talents to Alabama."

Besides all of the football recruiting, I had a full-paid academic scholarship offer from Princeton. One of my high school English teachers was a Princeton graduate who must have cared deeply about my education. She had sent off my tests and transcripts to Princeton, and they had responded with a full-paid academic scholarship.

There was so much to consider and I had no idea how to make this decision of where to go to college. I had never been through this type of situation before, of course. But worse than that, neither had anyone else. There were no Black players in Montgomery that had gone through something like this. There was no one I could look to for unbiased advice. No one who could tell me what pitfalls to avoid.

I really needed guidance from someone who only cared about helping me. Even though I tried, I never felt like I found that help. Even our coaches—all good men—could not help but think about the fact that they were getting job offers from colleges.

Finally, in desperation, I decided to go talk to one of the local ministers about it. He immediately tried to persuade me to go to one particular school. I said, "Okay, what did they offer you?" He said, "Well, they didn't offer me anything, but some people would make a contribution to the church if you went there."

SOME UNBIASED ADVICE

It was clear that if I were going to get any honest feedback and advice at all, it would come from only one place—my parents. People might have tried to offer them things to help persuade me. Fortunately, my dad did not need anything. He had a house. He had cars. He was not rich, but he would have probably laughed at a job offer—he already had about 10 jobs! Running his own businesses was more than enough work for him.

My mother was incorruptible. She only cared about what was best for her children. There was no way to appeal to her selfish motives, because there's no way to appeal to something that didn't exist.

In general, my parents consistently advised me to figure out where *I wanted to play*. So I began focusing heavily on that question. USC, Notre Dame, Oklahoma, and Tennessee were at the forefront of my mind. After some time, the answer was clear. The number one place I *wanted to play* football was for the University of Southern California.

First and foremost, they ran an I-formation out of the backfield. The "I-formation" refers to a vertical alignment of quarterback, fullback, and running back. This type of offense tends to put great emphasis on the running game, and the tailback in particular.

USC had already had several great running backs in its recent history, including Mike Garrett and O.J. Simpson—both of whom had won the Heisman. At the time I was being recruited, Sam Cunningham was also running roughshod over defenses all across the country. This included a historic game against Alabama.

Sam was a backup fullback coming into that season opener against Alabama. He had a breakout performance with 12 rushes for 135 yards and 2 touchdowns—not bad for a second-string fullback. USC also won that game in dominating fashion, beating Alabama 42-21. All of USC's touchdowns were scored by Black players. At that time, there were no Black players on Alabama's varsity roster.

Alabama had technically integrated by signing Wilbur Jackson to the team in 1970. But there were still a lot of question marks about how this integration thing was going to work out for Alabama football. There was a lot of resistance from some circles.

At that time, college football did not allow freshmen to play on the varsity team. So college football had freshmen teams that played each other on Friday nights, normally to much smaller crowds. That setup meant Alabama still did not have any Black players on its varsity team. So it was not unnoticed when USC came to Legion Field and decimated Bear Bryant's all-white team.

That game is now widely cited as being crucial for advancing the cause of integration at Alabama, but racial issues were not the driving force behind my desire to go to school at USC. It was strictly a football decision for me. USC had been extremely successful in running that I-formation offense, and they had done so for a number of years. I loved that deep I-formation, and it definitely played to my strengths.

However, there was one huge problem.

Back then, there was no ESPN. There might have been two USC games per year that would be televised where my family lived. Realistically, my family might be able to make the trip once per year to Southern California to see me play. So at most, they would be able to see me play three times per year if I went to USC.

That pretty quickly ruled out USC for me, even though I really wanted to play there.

Notre Dame was another very prestigious football program that was recruiting me heavily. My decision-making process might sound overly simplistic, but this is the truth of the matter. I quickly determined that I could not play for Notre Dame because it was just too cold up there. Extreme cold weather was not something I was prepared to deal with.

Tennessee was another school on my short list. I loved Coach Bill Battle, who was and is a wonderful human being. When you meet Bill Battle, you know that he cares about you as a person. That made him a very effective recruiter. A young football player could not meet Coach Battle without knowing that he was very genuine, and he cared very much about what was best for you.

Coach Battle had recruited Condredge Holloway along with just about every other major program in the country. While a lot of schools wanted Condredge on their team, some of the other coaches would not commit to letting him play quarterback. There had never been a Black quarterback in the SEC before, so Bill Battle and Tennessee seemed very much ahead of the curve in regard to the integration issue.

I could have very easily ended up at Tennessee. Playing for Bill Battle definitely appealed to me, and playing alongside Condredge would have been great as well. But when I went to Knoxville for a recruiting visit, I just decided that I hated orange. They had orange *everything*. Orange buses. Orange benches around the city. I mean, even the streets were orange!

I just couldn't stand all that orange. Tennessee was out.

When I got back from my visit, I remember my mother asking me how it went. I said, "Oh, it was great. They were really nice to me. Great people."

"So you're thinking about going there?"

"Oh, no way. I'm not thinking about going there at all."

"Why?" she seemed puzzled.

"I just couldn't stand all that orange. There was orange everywhere. It's just so ugly. I hated looking at it all the time."

She was skeptical, "No . . . that's not it. They were ugly to you, weren't they? Did they say racist things to you?"

I assured her, "No, Mom. Everyone there was wonderful. They're like the greatest people in the world. I just really hated looking at the orange. It's overwhelming."

She still couldn't believe anyone would make a decision

based on a team color, but I was telling the truth. The orange just drove me crazy.

Looking back, that whole thing seems pretty funny. But now I believe that even when things don't make much sense at all, God is working through all of the details to bring about His purpose.

Oklahoma was another school that had a distance problem. That put them in the same boat as Southern Cal.

At that point, there were only two realistic options left: Alabama and Auburn. Both of those schools were heavily recruiting me, and because they were both in state, people all around me were constantly trying to persuade me to go to one of those schools.

Again, I found myself in a place of desperation when it came to making this decision. I had thought earnestly about where I *wanted* to play, but the one place I really wanted to play was ruled out for geographic reasons. Besides ruling out USC, I had been able to eliminate some other places, but I still had not been able to make a choice.

ANYWHERE BUT ALABAMA

So I went back to my parents. This time, I wanted their honest opinion for where *they thought* I should play.

I'll never forget what my mother said to me that day. She and my dad were both on the same page, and she spoke up for the two of them.

"You can go anywhere you want to go. You can play football, or you can go to Princeton and pursue academics. It's really your decision. But if you're asking *us* where you should go, the only thing we will say is that you definitely *should not go* to Alabama."

This was not a devastating blow to me by any stretch.

Over the years, many people have come up to me and said things like, "Wow, growing up in Montgomery, you must have dreamed of playing for Bear Bryant. That must have been so awesome to be able to live out a dream like that."

Hardly.

It's not that we had any sort of hatred for Alabama or Bear Bryant. But Black kids in Alabama did not grow up dreaming of playing for the Crimson Tide because it was not an option. You might as well have said, "You must have grown up dreaming about living on Mars one day."

It just wasn't in the field of possibilities.

Prior to 1970, never once in my life growing up as a young man in Alabama did I have any thought or dream of playing for Bear Bryant. It was not conceivable.

Pretty much every white kid in Alabama grew up dreaming of playing for Bear Bryant. He was a legend. But Black kids didn't even think about it.

We watched their games because that was often the only football on TV on a Saturday. Pure love for the sport might drive us to watch the games. I would kind of pull for Alabama over Auburn when they played, so it was not like we hated these teams. We just didn't feel like we were a part of their world.

So while I had no animosity toward Bear Bryant or Alabama, I really did not have any sense of loyalty or internal pull to play for "the home team."

My parents solidified that notion by explaining their position further.

My mother stated plainly, "You can play anywhere. But I personally saw that man [Bear Bryant] stand there on national TV and say, 'I will never recruit a Black player at

Alabama.' I heard the words come out of his mouth. I believe he's a racist. So we want this to be your decision, but our only rule is that you cannot play at Alabama."

Their statements were true.

In the 1960s, Bear Bryant had refused to recruit Black players. In 1963, Alabama Governor George Wallace—a rabid segregationist at that time—had infamously made his "stand in the schoolhouse door" to prevent the first African American students from entering. Wallace had utilized the national guard in making his stand.

President Kennedy responded by federalizing the national guard, and then giving the guard orders to compel Wallace to stand down. It's worth noting that years later, Wallace turned away from racism and asked everyone to forgive him for his previous actions. However, the "segregation forever" attitude largely defined the environment in Alabama in the 1960s, a time in which Coach Bryant had come to prominence with three national championships over a 5-year period.

That's what we saw happening at Alabama while we were growing up. Coach Bryant may have been a great coach, but we had no personal or emotional connection to the program. And we had plenty of reason to be suspect of them.

Still, they were in-state, so the geography problem would have been solved by playing there. Auburn was in-state as well, but they weren't exactly free of racial problems. Like Alabama, they were just starting to integrate.

Being a Black football player at either school seemed like a very risky proposition. Would I be treated fairly as a player? How would they treat me as a person? There were a lot of question marks. At the same time, it was very clear that there were *a lot* of people at both schools who *really* wanted me to play at these schools.

I couldn't completely rule them out yet—they were just so close to home. They ran the I-formation in the backfield. And they had very strong football programs with loads of success in the recent past, especially at Alabama. But with my parents telling me that they would only recommend one place I should never play, Alabama certainly felt like a long shot.

Enter Bear Bryant.

6

PLAYING FOR BEAR BRYANT

I n addition to the advice of my parents, there were a lot of voices in the Black community trying to dissuade me from going to Alabama. People at the Black colleges would try to appeal to my personal motives by saying things like, "You don't need to go to that white school. There won't be any other Black people on campus. They won't let you go to their parties. They're not gonna let you date their white girls, so there won't be any girls for you to date. You'll be miserable if you go there."

Others would try to make some kind of moral argument that Black talent should benefit Black colleges rather than "the white schools." They tried to put the future of Black education on my shoulders by saying things like, "Talented Black players have to stay with the Black schools in order to keep them viable." Still others would point out that the Black colleges send plenty of players to the NFL, so there would be no long-term professional disadvantage to playing at a Black college.

Some of these arguments were persuasive.

But as I mentioned before, I had felt from the time that God took me to Robert E. Lee that He had a calling on my life for the cause of integration. In light of that, I had to at least consider Alabama. Throughout the recruiting process, I had kept in contact with people at Alabama.

However, when it became clear that my mother would not be changing her mind on me playing at Alabama, I went ahead and called the person who had been most active in recruiting me.

"I can't come."

"Why not?"

"Well, my mom says she saw Bear Bryant go on TV and state that he would never recruit a Black player. So she believes he's a racist. She said she knows he said it, that she heard the words come out of his mouth. There's just no way. I can't come to Alabama."

The news quickly made its way around the coaching staff at Alabama.

After a short time I got a call back from the recruiter.

"Bear says that's unacceptable," the recruiter explained, before making a somewhat surprising request. "Ralph, can I talk to your mother?"

"Um, sure."

So they tell her the same thing, "Coach Bryant says that's an unacceptable position. He still believes your son should come to Alabama. Alabama wants your son on the team. Alabama needs your son on the team. Coach Bryant wants to know, What can he do to change your position on this?"

"He needs to come to Montgomery, look me in the eye, and tell me he didn't say that," she stated in a matter of fact way.

"Okay . . . well, that might be hard to do. But okay, I'll tell him."

A day or two later we got another phone call. They only wanted to know one thing. "When would be a good time for Coach Bryant to come?"

My mother responded, "Now, he can't just come down here. He has to come down here, look me in the eye, and tell me he didn't say that."

I don't know if that was my mother's way of making her point. She knew he had said it, so she wasn't leaving them any realistic option for continuing to recruit me. But Coach Bryant decided to take her up on the invitation anyway.

They assured her, "We told him what you said, and he wants to come."

She replied, "Okay, Friday evening at 4:00."

"He'll be there."

It didn't take long for word to get out. Bear Bryant was coming to Montgomery, Alabama. That was a big deal. Not only that, but Bear Bryant was coming to Newtown to visit a Black kid. That was a *very big* deal.

By Friday evening, there was a lot of buzz around town for Coach Bryant's visit. People from the neighborhood were out in the streets. A white local police captain, Captain King, was friends with my dad. He wanted to meet Coach Bryant, so he was there in his squad car.

Captain King was the first one to meet Coach Bryant when he stepped out of the car. Captain King was a well-respected man in our community. It was surreal watching him act like a star-struck sports fan.

"Coach Bryant, it's such an honor to have you here. I've watched this kid grow up. I watched him. I helped raise him. This is *my* kid, you're gonna love him."

Captain King was so honored to be a part of that day.

Coach Bryant had Raymond Perdue and Coach Richard Williamson with him, and as I recall, they were all wearing jackets and ties. My family members were all dressed in clothing that was nice, but short of our Sunday best. As the coaches walked up toward the door, my mother came out of the front door and stood on the porch. She greeted Coach Bryant.

Bear Bryant had a larger than life persona, but at 6' 4", he also had an imposing physical stature. Not to be outmatched, my mother stood up in the doorway and began talking to Coach Bryant while he was still down a foot or two at the porch level. This put them precisely on eye-to-eye level.

So there they were face to face, not so close as to violate normal personal space, but close enough to be zeroed in on each other—almost like no one else was even around.

My mother began respectfully addressing Coach Bryant. "It's such an honor to have you here Coach Bryant. We're thrilled that you would take time to come to our home here in Montgomery. It's truly an honor to have such an outstanding coach as yourself here at our home . . . "

"Thank you, Ma—"

Before he could respond, her next sentence seemed to steal all of the positive energy out of the entire crowd of people.

" . . . But I'd like to know *why* you're here . . . "

She didn't waste any time getting to the point.

" . . . because I know I saw you state on national TV that you would never recruit a Black player . . . "

Coach Bryant waited patiently for his chance to speak.

" . . . and if I'm not mistaken, this young man standing right here is Black . . . "

Even the most brash of human beings would have felt a little uncomfortable standing nearby at that moment, but my mother never missed a beat.

"... So why are you here?"

Dead silence.

There was a pregnant pause, seemingly long, but what stood out the most was the absolute silence. All afternoon leading up to his arrival, the atmosphere had been electrically charged. Now we were all just hoping and praying that we could avoid any kind of ugly scene. This did not seem to be going well at all.

Coach Bryant never flinched. He looked her in the eye the entire time. And when he was sure it was his turn to talk, he responded humbly, but with conviction.

"Yes Ma'am ... "

"... I did say it."

There was another pause. Everyone was very anxious as to what he would say next.

"And I did mean it."

Okay, this is really not going well. How can this situation ever turn for the good? The visit was starting to seem like an absolute disaster.

"But I was *wrong.*"

Whew! Okay, now maybe we're getting somewhere good. Let's see if this thing gets turned around.

Coach Bryant continued, "And I'm still not here to recruit a Black player. I'm here to recruit a football player. And your son happens to be a very good football player."

You could feel the tension ease. Everyone breathed a sigh of relief. The collective assessment of the situation was, "Okay, he said he was wrong. That's good. He's admitting that his racism was wrong." That seemed to be everyone's reaction—with one important exception.

"No. That's not acceptable. That's not enough. You don't have any Black players up there ... " My mother shot back at Coach Bryant.

Technically, that wasn't true. Wilbur Jackson had gotten a scholarship offer from Alabama the year before. He was a freshman at the time this conversation was happening. So again, in those days, that meant he was on the freshman team. He was not on the varsity football team yet. But my mother was only speaking in general terms, as you might if you were referring to Montana by saying, "There are no Black people there." Technically there are a few, but it's an extremely low percentage.

My mother continued, " ... so who's going to take care of him while he's there?"

Somewhat stoically, but with earnestness and sincerity, Coach Bryant responded, "I will take care of him. I will be his father away from home. I will make sure he's taken care of."

Each time she shot over a tough question, Coach Bryant came back with a good response. But before anyone could start to enjoy a sense of relief at the tension being eased, my mother would shoot right back.

"That *sounds* good, but you can't be with him all the time. You can't be with him when he walks across the campus. When he's going to class. When he's out and about as a young person trying to live life. They're gonna be ugly to him. They're gonna call him names."

Coach Bryant didn't sugarcoat anything, "Yes Ma'am. They probably will. But if I didn't think he was man enough to deal with that kind of thing, I wouldn't be here."

My mother wasn't about to let up. "Again, that *sounds* good. But you don't have any Black players yet. How are you going to treat Ralph? Are you going to treat him the same that you treat everybody else?"

Coach Bryant wasn't anything if he wasn't honest. After a moment of reflection, he told her exactly what he intended to do. "No Ma'am. I will not treat him the same that I treat everyone else, but I will treat him fair."

My mother's interrogation lasted for a few more questions, and I wish I could remember the details. But suffice it to say, they all followed that same pattern of her challenging Coach Bryant on the idea of me playing for Alabama as a young Black man.

That whole time, no one else said a word. It was just Coach Bryant and my mother, face to face, eye to eye, hashing out the ground rules for my future. It seemed like neither of them blinked the whole time. Neither of them looked at anyone else for help. Neither of them struggled to find words. They were both zeroed in, fully confident, and fully engaged in discussing this very important matter.

At that moment, there was a break in the standoff. I can't remember exactly what triggered it, but what I do remember is that all of a sudden, my mother's entire demeanor shifted. She went from being the stern, protective mother hen to being a polite host. I suppose Coach Bryant had answered the race-related questions to my mother's satisfaction, because her interrogation was suddenly over.

"Oh, Coach Bryant, would you like to come in? Can I get you a glass of tea?"

So Coach Bryant and the rest of his group came inside. My entire family went in and we all sat down in the living room. The whole visit lasted for about an hour and the rest of the visit was relatively light. From that time forward, they talked about things like living arrangements, meals, and practice schedules. Coach Bryant talked about his coaching philosophy. There were no other tense moments that I can recall. Everyone had moved on from the race issue, at least in regard to that day's discussion.

Years later, during an interview, Coach Bryant recalled the meeting with my mother. He said that what he remembered the most about my mother was that she did something no other parents had done. Whenever Coach Bryant met with parents, they always asked him if he would guarantee playing time for their son. Would he guarantee a certain position, and that kind of thing.

What he recalled about my mother was that she never once asked him to guarantee me a certain position or playing time. She did ask Coach Bryant if *he would be fair* in letting me *compete* for playing time. He assured her that he would. But every other question she had for him that day was in regard to academics. According to Coach Bryant, my mother was almost totally focused on my education and making sure I fulfilled my academic potential.

That must have been pretty rare, because Coach Bryant said that this was what stood out to him the most about her. He also said that her position—prioritizing my long-term success in life over short-term success in football—caused him to respect her. It also made him more personally determined to do the same, that is, to prioritize my long term personal success over football.

Whatever happened that day, whatever connection Coach Bryant and my mother had, the results of their meeting were undeniable.

When we sat down for breakfast the next day, my mother began to explain their position to me.

"Well, Ralph, your father and I talked about it. This is still your decision. We want you to make this decision, and we trust you to make the right decision. But *if it were up to us*, we think you should seriously consider going to Alabama and playing for Bear Bryant."

My mother was not easily influenced by anyone, but Coach Bryant's power of influence was that great.

CHALLENGES AS A PLAYER

I was a pure out and out tailback. Whenever I'm asked to reflect on my career, I always tell people that I was extremely gifted with the football in my hand. However, when the football was not in my hand, it was more challenging for me.

To be totally honest, I would not describe myself as having been a great football player. I was great at scoring. I was great at racking up yards. But I really struggled with other aspects of the game, like blocking and tackling.

Being a tailback, the tackling wasn't much of a problem. But it was a big problem that I couldn't block.

It wasn't that I didn't want to block. I tried to learn. This was just a skill that eluded me for whatever reason.

There was another major issue that came up shortly after I made the commitment to play at Alabama. Bear Bryant had been sold on the wishbone formation for his offense during the offseason.

One of the major factors in my decision to go to Alabama was that they ran an I-formation out of the backfield. I would have been playing tailback, which meant the I-formation would have played to my strengths. In a wishbone formation, you have two tailbacks and both of them spend more time blocking than they do running the ball. So the wishbone formation didn't play to my strengths nearly as much as an I-formation would have.

Once Coach Bryant made the decision, the assumption was that I could learn to block and thereby prosper in a wishbone offense. The optimism inspired by my pure running talent was enough to give me as much chance as anyone to contribute.

One of my major gifts was vision. To this day, my peripheral vision is exceptional. Without turning my head, I can see and perceive a lot of what's going on around me. So I had the ability to see where I needed to go, and what cuts I needed to make. That strength is good for a running back to have no matter what formation they're running, but the most benefit would have come through running a deep, pro-set I-formation.

For many of us, the choice to move to the wishbone felt like a strange decision. Remember, they had recruited me as the number one running back in the South, the third-rated running back in the nation, and a high school All-American. I was a pure runner.

They had also recruited Robert Fraley, who was the number one passing quarterback in the nation. Robert wasn't built for rushing. He was a pure passer. But to play wishbone, the quarterback really needs to be able to run the ball. The switch didn't feel like it made a lot of sense, especially to Robert and me.

Robert saw himself in the same light as Joe Namath, Kenny Stabler, and Pat Trammell. Those quarterbacks had all seen great success at Alabama dropping back into the pocket and lighting up defenses. I saw myself like Johnny Musso, running behind a fullback and getting the ball 20-30 times per game.

But Alabama was now running the wishbone. We could hope for it to change, but we could not change it.

They actually told Robert and me about the change as soon as we showed up for football camp. They called Robert, myself, and one other player into Coach Bryant's office. We were told, "Guys, we have a change. We're excited about it, and it's going to work really well. You're going to fit into it. But we're changing from a pro set to a wishbone."

There's no way to overstate the importance of that decision. It just was not good at all for my style of play. Robert was very discouraged too. My honest assessment is that it was a particularly crushing blow for him. He was a phenomenal drop back passer, not a run-pitch option QB.

We just were not wishbone players. In spite of that, we both resolved to do our best.

DEALING WITH INJURIES

In spite of the challenges, my start at Alabama was not that bad. During freshman football, I managed to lead the team in yards and touchdowns, and made the All-SEC Freshman team. But the coaches constantly harped on pretty much every other aspect of my game. I remember being in the film room, where they would be watching the results of our most recent scrimmage. They'd say things like, "Okay, Ralph, you scored five touchdowns, but you also missed five blocks. And three of those times, you never even touched the defender!"

At the end of my freshman year, I had a really good spring practice season. There was plenty of excitement about my prospects at the start of my sophomore year. Wilbur

Jackson—the first ever Black football player at Alabama—was a starting tailback. Wilbur had come in the year before I did, so he was now a junior. Wilbur went on to be drafted 9th overall in the first round of the 1974 NFL draft. He spent 8 seasons in the NFL, playing for the 49ers and later the Redskins.

At the start of my sophomore year, I was first in line on the depth chart behind Wilbur. Because we were running the wishbone, we had two starting tailbacks. Joe LaBue was the other starting tailback that year.

Even though I was backing up a stalwart of the Alabama offense, I was set to get plenty of playing time that year. It was time to make my debut on the big stage, suiting up for the first time ever for the Alabama Crimson Tide varsity team. But the very last scrimmage before the first game, I separated my shoulder.

I would be out for 3-4 weeks.

This is the other major challenge I ran into while playing college football. It felt like I just could not stay completely healthy during my time at Alabama.

Injuries plagued Robert Fraley as well, as he had three shoulder surgeries during his time at Alabama. It felt like the deck was stacked against us both.

When you're competing for playing time, injuries don't just knock you down for the time that you're officially sitting out of practice. There can be a lingering effect. When you come back into the rotation in practice, someone else now has a 3-4 week advantage on you. On top of that, you're trying to get back into shape quickly, and you're likely to be timid about the possibility of getting reinjured.

It's obviously not impossible to overcome injuries and get back into full swing. But it can be challenging, especially when you're competing against 4 years' worth of the nation's top recruits (freshmen had now joined the varsity squad since the NCAA had made a rule change and done away with freshman football forever after 1971).

The problem was amplified for me, because as I mentioned, I could not stay completely healthy for very long.

Overall, my sophomore year was a net positive. I was able to stay healthy enough to make significant contributions to the program. I ended the year with 35 rushing attempts, and 1 catch for a 48-yard touchdown. Just for comparison purposes, Wilbur had 37 rushing attempts and one touchdown in his sophomore year. So all in all, there was still reason for hope.

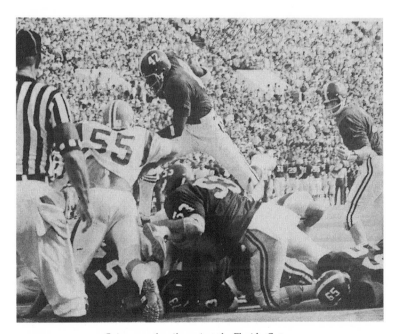

Going over the pile against the Florida Gators.

But the injuries continued to plague me. During my time

at Alabama, I ended up separating my shoulder three different times. My jaw was broken. I had broken ribs. My wrist was broken. There were relatively minor injuries, but all of them had the effect of slowing me down and hindering my progress as a player.

It felt like any kind of injury you could name, I had it at some point. This basically resulted in me staying out of the starting lineup.

In the end, I just never blossomed into the player that everyone hoped I would.

The irony is that my friend, Mike Washington, was not that heavily recruited by Alabama. We were very good friends, and we really wanted to continue playing together at the college level. To hear him tell it, Alabama only gave him a scholarship because of me. But he ended up being an All-American at Alabama, and going on to have a very successful career in the NFL.

You never know for sure how things are going to turn out in life, so you might as well make the most of every opportunity. Do your best, and then leave the final results up to God.

Try to have some fun along the way, too.

In the end, I can say that it was an honor to wear the crimson jersey. I am very thankful for my career at Alabama. I often played on special teams and even scored some touchdowns here and there in spite of the challenges I faced as a player. I was blessed with the honor of contributing to four SEC championships and one National Championship during my four years at Alabama, and I am forever grateful that I had the opportunity to do so.

7

RACIAL PROBLEMS AT ALABAMA

Whenever sports writers and reporters have contacted me over the years, they usually end up a little bit disappointed. The reason is that they're wanting to hear about all of the racial problems and challenges I experienced during my time as a football player at Alabama. For the most part, we just weren't having those kinds of experiences.

Every now and then, you might hear a student say the n-word out loud—normally when there was quite a bit of distance between us. Some people on campus were still racist for sure. There were times when a student might say the n-word loudly to *make sure* you heard it, even though you were walking on the other side of the street.

I had to deal with things like that every once in a while. My approach was just to let it roll off of my back like water off of a duck's feathers. There's no way I was going to let a few messed up people ruin my college experience or my future. That being said, I do acknowledge that it was not easy or fun hearing those kinds of things. But fortunately, football life was almost completely free of race-related problems.

Truth be told, there was one incident that involved Mike Washington. There was a white player on the team who was racist. Mike got into an argument with this white player, and that player said some racist things to Mike. The other player was off the team in very short order.

That is the only race-related incident involving athletes—that I'm aware of—which occurred during my years at Alabama.

While I understand that it would make for a more interesting read to hear tales of racism on the team, it just wasn't there. If any of our team members were harboring racism in their hearts, they did a good job of hiding it. The truth is that Bear Bryant had laid down the law on this issue, and for the most part, people did not dare to defy him.

Whatever mistakes the man might have made in the past, he definitely corrected them. For anyone to treat us in a disrespectful or discriminatory way because of race was unthinkable on Bryant's football team.

Besides that, sports has a way of uniting people. The concept of "teammate" often overcomes any hangups a person might initially have about race or background.

This next story illustrates that principle quite well.

TEAMMATES

Paul W. Bryant Hall is a dormitory where the football players live while on the University of Alabama campus. Back when I was there, the male basketball players also lived at Bryant Hall.

The dorm is right next to Fraternity Row. So there are

fraternity houses running beside and behind Bryant Hall. For the most part, these fraternity members were very friendly with the football players.

They loved having football players come to their parties, but it was generally only the white players that went. The social scene just wasn't very integrated yet.

One time, in the middle of the afternoon on a Saturday, a nearby fraternity was having a party. Some of the white players, maybe 8-10 total, had walked over. I was walking by, along with a few other Black athletes, on our way to go grab some food. I can't recall for sure who else was with me.

The white players who were outside at this party called for us to stop and have a beer with them. We thought, well, there's 8-10 of "our guys" over there, meaning football players. It seemed safe enough in light of that, so we agreed and then walked across the street to have a beer.

It wasn't very long before one of the fraternity guys came out of the house and said, "Why are *they* here? They're not welcome here." Everyone sort of stopped and stared, maybe in disbelief.

So he got louder, "We don't want them here!"

Then he dropped the n-word.

It did not take long for our teammates to respond.

Of the white players who were there, I can recall for sure John Hannah and Jim Krapf. Both of those guys were absolutely huge offensive lineman. John was a future NFL guard who stood at 6-2, and weighed 265 lbs. Jim was a center. He was 6 foot, 240 lbs, and like John, he was an All-American. But Jim also happened to be the SEC heavyweight wrestling champion.

He just wasn't the guy to mess with for any reason, but

especially not for this reason. So that was the man's first mistake.

Jim Krapf was instantly furious with this guy. He was so mad, he just immediately burst into a full sprint toward the man. The man, visibly frightened, began to run from Jim. But Jim kept chasing.

The man managed to make it into a porta-potty that had been brought in for the party. That was his second mistake.

Jim was as strong as three mules. He picked up that porta-potty with the man locked inside. Another lineman—I can't remember which one—ran to the other side and helped Jim flip the porta-potty all the way upside down.

The man was inside, obviously terrified, and now covered in an absolutely disgusting mess. From Jim's perspective, he was just getting warmed up. It was clear that he was not done with the man. So the man held onto that door for dear life and kept himself locked inside.

As I recall, that was the end of the incident, at least from our perspective. Someone must have gotten our guys to calm down and leave it be, because I don't remember ever seeing the man come out of there.

We all had a good laugh and then went back to having a fun day. I guess the fraternity member spent the rest of his day trying to wash off the stench.

To this day, Jim is an outstanding guy. The way he stood up for us that day was indicative of the overall attitude that most players on the team had for one another. We were teammates, and that bond superseded any other loyalties or social pressures we might have been tempted to give into.

A COMMON EXPERIENCE

I was not the only one who had this type of experience playing sports at Alabama—one that was largely free of any kind of racial problem. When I first got to Alabama, there were two other Black players on the football team, Wilbur Jackson and John Mitchell. Wilbur had been the first Black player to accept a scholarship offer from Alabama. However, that was in the days when freshmen couldn't play on the varsity squad.

John was a junior college transfer to Alabama. Showing up in time for the 1971 season, John was actually the first African American player to suit up for the varsity squad at Alabama. That's why you might see some articles which herald John as Alabama's first Black player, and some which give Wilbur that same honor.

What I was part of, technically, was the first full Black recruiting class at Alabama. Yes, there were only three of us. But, it's enough to call us a recruiting class. Wilbur had been recruited as the first and only Black scholarship football player during the fall of 1969, and he signed on for the 1970 season as a freshman. John had later transferred to Alabama in the spring of 1970.

It was almost like Alabama was still dipping their toe in the water.

But with our class, their intention was clear. They were recruiting Black players all over the state, and they actually signed three of us: Mike Washington, Sylvester Croom, and me. Whether you like the designation of "first Black recruiting class" or not, there's no denying that I was one of the first Black football players at Alabama, along with Wilbur, John, Mike, and Sylvester.

Just like I had been one of the first Black players at Robert E. Lee, I was now one of the first at Alabama. And being "one of the first" was a pattern that would follow me throughout my life.

Around the same time we were being recruited and signing on to become the first group of Black football players, Alabama was also enjoying its first Black basketball players. Wendell Hudson had become the first ever African American scholarship athlete at the University of Alabama in 1969. I've had the privilege to know Wendell over the years, and he became one of my best friends. He was recently honored by having his jersey retired at Alabama—their first and only jersey retirement.

The weekend of that event, I was there along with Sylvester Croom. I don't presume to speak for these other men. But in being around all of these guys over the years, I'm comfortable in giving you *my understanding* that we're all consistent in describing similar experiences.

In fact, we sometimes joke about what I mentioned before—that reporters don't want to talk to us about our experiences at Alabama. They think they do. But when we tell them the truth—that we had positive experiences devoid of racial problems—they quickly lose interest. They just can't imagine that no one was calling us the n-word or treating us unfairly.

I personally knew African American players who were not having the same experience at other colleges that had recently integrated. Some of the guys I had known in high school were routinely being called the n-word during practice—and not just by other players. Some of them were actually called the n-word in football practice by their own coaches!

Say what you want about Alabama. They waited way too long to integrate, and they were wrong for that. But when they did integrate, they did it right.

BUSINESS SCHOOL IS TOO HARD FOR YOU

There was one major problem that occurred when I first arrived at Alabama. For the most part, everyone treated me well. I believe that everyone was sincerely doing their best to treat me as good as they knew how.

But there were undoubtedly still racial prejudices that lingered in people's hearts and minds. That kind of thing doesn't just vanish overnight—even if everyone is trying their best to be free of it. In my experience, racial prejudices, obstacles, and barriers are intentionally broken down and overcome.

My first experience in trying to register for classes revealed some of those prejudices and obstacles. We had to go to Foster Auditorium—the same place where George Wallace had made his infamous stand in the schoolhouse door—to meet with our academic advisors, select a major, and register for classes.

Football players had a special registration session before everyone else. We arrived on campus before the other students so that we could attend football camp. Besides being there earlier, we also needed scheduling priority to make sure we could get our required classes at time slots that would enable us to do workouts, attend practice sessions, and meet other team requirements.

One of the football coaches was our academic advisor, and another coach was our dorm adviser, so they had input on our decision making. They were also supposed to help the freshmen get the classes they needed at the times they needed.

I came in and sat down for my meeting with the coach that was an academic advisor. He asked what major I was planning to choose.

"I want to go to the business school," I mentioned in a casual tone, not aware that my request would be problematic in any way.

"No, that's not an option. Our players have two options. You can major in PE in the College of Education, or you can major in social work. Those are the two opportunities. The professors in those schools are used to working with football players, working around our schedules, and they're ready to help you succeed.

"We have counselors and tutors in those schools that know the material in those programs very well, and they work closely to help the football players academically. So we can get you through those schools with no problem," he explained, trying his best to sound convincing.

But the look on my face communicated that I was not buying into his sales pitch. "I understand what you're saying, but that's not what I want to do."

There's no doubt that going to business school meant serious academic work. No matter which specific major you choose, going to business school involves taking classes in accounting, calculus, economics, statistics, and operations management, among other things. I knew I could have taken an easier route, but that just didn't interest me.

At that point, my coach attempted to persuade me by pointing out that, "This is just what the athletes do." There were even three basketball players at that same meeting, and they had already signed up for the programs this coach was trying to sell me on. I wasn't trying to be difficult, but I had no interest in coaching or doing social work.

"I want to go to business school," I asserted confidently.

While Auburn was known for its technical programs like science and engineering, Alabama was well-known for having a great business school and a great law school. Those were really the pride of the university at the time in terms of academics.

"No, you can't go," was the matter-of-fact response I received this time. The coach added, "It's too hard. We can't risk you failing."

Now we were getting to the truth of the matter.

The other coach had joined the discussion at this point, and they began to get impatient with me, "Ralph, pick one of these two programs."

I was now being given a direct order. In general, I'm not one to defy direct orders from my football coaches, but I was not about to budge.

"I'm not picking one of those two. I'm going to business school," was my prompt reply. It was a little uncomfortable to be in that position. Football camp had only started two or three weeks prior, so I was brand new on campus—a Black freshman football player defying his white coaches.

Finally, one of the coaches furrowed his brow and asserted, "No, son. We've been told from the top that you cannot attend business school. So if you want to go to the business school, you're going to have to talk to Coach Bryant." When he said this, I could tell he thought that would be his final remark. No further intimidation would be necessary. The mere mention of Coach Bryant's authority would end the discussion right there, or so he thought.

Coach Bryant was bigger than life. You don't go to his

office asking for special requests after you've been told no. No one does that—especially not a Black freshman.

"That's fine. If I need to talk to Coach Bryant about this, then I'll go talk to Coach Bryant—because *I'm going* to the business school."

"No, you're not."

They were starting to get somewhat offended at my assertiveness by this point, but I did not back down. The more domineering they were in their approach toward me, the more confident and firm I was in my response.

"Yes, I am," was my final reply.

"Okay, well, this is *really* not a good decision for you. But if you really want to go talk to Coach Bryant, then that's what you'll do, young man."

A BARRIER IS BROKEN

The next morning, I had an appointment to see Coach Bryant. Coach Bryant had this old couch in his office that would sink way down when you sat on it. By contrast, his desk and chair sat up much higher than normal. Add to that the fact that he was 6′ 4″, and you almost felt like a child looking up at his dad.

After I sat down, Coach Bryant opened the discussion.

"Ralph, they tell me you don't want to go where we asked you to—you want to go to the business school."

"Yes sir. That's what I'd like to do and that's why I'm here."

"Well, now that's a hard school. Those folks push you really hard. Are you sure that you can do this, and that you want to do this?"

"Yes sir. Coach, I really want to do this. I want to go to the business school. So that's why I'm here—to ask you for permission to go to the business school." I had already made that much clear, but I was still being questioned, so I wasn't sure what else to do except repeat myself.

He shifted gears just a bit.

"Well, what do you want to do, Ralph? You obviously want to attend business school, so what is it that you want to be?"

"Coach, I really don't know what I want to be. I have no idea. I don't know what specific job I want. But I can tell you this. In the neighborhood where I grew up, all the men walked to work before the sun came up. Most of them wore overalls, and some of them wore the exact same thing every day. They all did manual labor, outside in the sun, or in a hot factory somewhere. So I can't tell you exactly what job I'm fighting for. But I can tell you that when I go to work, it will be after the sun comes up. And I'll be headed to an office somewhere. And I'll be wearing a suit and tie."

His tone softened. I dare say I saw a grin almost crack one side of his face before he shifted back to a serious, thoughtful expression.

"Well, you seem motivated. It seems like you have a plan. It's *gonna* be hard—now, you understand that?"

"Yes sir. I understand that."

"You're gonna have to study. And you're gonna have to work hard."

"Yes sir. I understand that."

"Okay, well, you seem to have the right mindset about it. You understand what you're getting into, and you know where you want to go. I'm gonna let you do this . . . " he paused slightly before giving me his vote of confidence, " . . . and I know you'll do well."

"Coach, thank you. And yes sir, I understand."

Barriers are broken intentionally. I don't know if white players were ever told they couldn't go to the UA business school because it was "too hard." But I seriously doubt if there was ever any white player at UA *who also had an academic scholarship offer from Princeton*, that was told he couldn't go to business school because it was "too hard."

There was a barrier. A little persistence, a little intentionality, and a significant amount of personal ambition were all that was needed to break the barrier.

The truth is, the business school was challenging. My coaches weren't lying or exaggerating about that. But like anything else in life, you step up and you meet the challenge. I made some lifelong friends in fellow players Ricky Davis and Robert Fraley. We were already friends from being on the team together. But during our four years, we had every single business school class together.

I'll never forget how Ricky's dad was extremely nice and supportive of all of us. He was a Birmingham area banker, and a great man to know. Ricky is still a wonderful friend. Robert was also a great human being and a great friend.

Unfortunately, Robert passed away much too early at the age of 46. It was 1999, and Robert had become a very successful sports agent. While on a flight with pro golfer Payne Stewart, the plane went down in a very mysterious crash, and there were no survivors. Robert passed much too early, but he had clearly benefited from all that time in the business school, and later on in the law school.

Ricky also benefited. Even though his next stop after Alabama was the NFL, and then later on law school, his business acumen served him well. He became a very successful sports agent too. In fact, he and Robert ended up breaking into the profession together, after having a conversation and deciding "it couldn't be that hard."[1]

The business school has also served me very well, and I'll share more detail in later chapters. But the point is that I could have easily missed the opportunity. It would have been considerably less trouble to just concede, and take the educational opportunities I was being offered by my coaches.

Instead, I chose to persevere. It was almost purely out of self-interest, but a barrier was broken in the process. I hope and believe that no other player was ever told that a particular college would be too hard for him just because he was Black.

Years later, I would serve for six years on UA's Culverhouse College of Business Board of Visitors—an advisory board designed to enhance the College's ability to accomplish its mission by making connections across the business world. So not only did I make it through the business school as a student, I came back to serve in an advisory role. Once you break the first barrier, there are still plenty more to be broken!

8

COACH BRYANT'S PROMISES FULFILLED

There are a few more things I'd like to share about Coach Bryant. He is an intriguing personality for several reasons. This is the man who said he would never recruit a Black player. On the other hand, he is a man who recognized his wrong and turned completely in the other direction.

He was also a man of his word.

The 1970s were a time of big cars, big shoes, and big hair. All of those things were probably important to college-aged men. But for me and some friends of mine, facial hair proved particularly important.

A MUSTACHE IS IMPORTANT

The football players at that time were not allowed to have facial hair. The reasoning, at least officially, was that it could interfere with healing time in the case of an injury like a busted lip or a busted chin. Whether that was the real reason or not, the rule was strictly enforced. Facial hair was not allowed.

Somewhere around the end of my freshman year, I decided to voice my concern about this very important matter.

I say that a bit tongue in cheek, and it's easy to laugh about it looking back. But at that time, a mustache was very much a sign of manhood—at least to all of the Black men I knew. The Jewish community has a Bar Mitzvah at the age of 13 to signify that a boy has become a man. Well, we grew mustaches as a sign of manhood in the Black community.

It was very unusual for someone to get to the 10th or 11th grade and not have a mustache. And to me personally, it was very important.

So one day I got together with Mike Washington and Sylvester Croom and began stirring the pot a little, "You know, we ought to be able to have a mustache."

I could see that maybe we shouldn't be able to have the long sideburns and the beard or a goatee. But I felt strongly that a mustache should be okay.

I continued, "We need to ask Coach Bryant for the right to grow a mustache, because it's really important."

Mike and Sylvester both seemed to agree, "Yeah, it's important in the Black neighborhood, but we're on a white team. Coach Bryant's not gonna let us do that."

I guess persistence is just a personality trait God gave me. It certainly seems to have served His purposes for my life. But sometimes it shows up in the most unexpected of situations.

"We don't know that," I interjected. "We need to go ask him."

I was resolute.

"No, we don't," was their collective response. "We don't need to be going into Coach Bryant's office for *anything*— especially not to talk about growing a mustache."

They were probably right. I mean, this was the offseason. It may have been right at the end of spring practice—usually not an opportune time for you to go bring up a grievance with your head coach.

I was undeterred. "Yes, we do. We ought to be able to grow a mustache. We're going to ask this man if we can grow a mustache."

So I got us a meeting. I think Mike and Sylvester both thought it was a little crazy, but they showed up anyway.

We sat down, and I explained that a mustache was very important in the Black community. I thoughtfully and carefully outlined the whole issue, explaining how, from the time a Black man is first able to grow a mustache, it's a very important sign of maturity for him. It tells everyone around him that he has become a man, so without it, he feels incomplete as a man. I think I even used the comparison to the Jewish Bar Mitzvah. Then I said, "As Black players, we would really like the right and the opportunity to grow a mustache."

He peered at me.

I held my ground by not flinching or looking away.

He was incredulous, "That's what yall want!?!"

Not a good first response, and it only got worse from there.

"That's what you called this meeting for? No! Get out of here."

That was the end of our meeting. There was no openness on the issue. There was no apology or explanation that it just couldn't be done. It was a definite, 100% "No" with a "how dare you waste my time" to boot.

So the semester ended. We all went home for the summer. When we came back, none of us were still thinking about mustaches. That topic was completely off the table.

But early in the fall semester, shortly after we all got back on campus, we got a phone call in the dorm. "Coach Bryant would like to meet with Ralph, Mike, and Sylvester tomorrow at 7 am."

Sylvester and Mike both looked at me and basically said, "What have you done?"

"Nothing. I haven't done anything."

"Come on now, we know it's you."

Sylvester had been raised in church from the time he was in diapers. His dad was a well-known minister, and also our team chaplain. Sylvester himself was always straitlaced. He was ruled out right off the bat. We knew he hadn't done anything wrong.

Mike usually wasn't one to slip up either.

That pretty much left me as the lone culprit, at least in everyone's mind. But I was sure I hadn't done anything wrong this time. We just couldn't figure it out.

When we got there the next morning, we were all scared to death because we still had no idea why we were there.

Then Coach Bryant began, "Gentlemen, last year you came to me and asked me about growing a mustache. I said no. But over the summer, I talked to several of my coaching friends, especially those who have had Black players for a long time.

"I talked to Ara Parseghian at Notre Dame. I talked to John McKay at Southern Cal. They both confirmed that in the Black community, a mustache is a really important symbol or rite of passage into manhood. They also confirmed that they allow their players to take part in that by growing a mustache. So I'm going to allow the Black players to grow a mustache. No sideburns. No beard. Just a mustache."

He only allowed the Black players to grow a mustache. No white player could grow one.

This is what Coach Bryant had meant when he told my mother he would not treat me like everyone else, but he would treat me fair. His response had been honest and thoughtful. Even though he did not have any particular issue in mind at the time he first said it, he had enough foresight to know that there might come a day—and a particular issue —where he would not treat me "the same." So his commitment was to treat me "fair" instead.

And he honored that commitment.

His word was obviously important enough to him that after throwing us out of his office in frustration—at an issue that he did not initially understand at all—he could not stop thinking about our conversation. He had to get to the bottom of it and determine whether we were being treated fairly or not. So that's what he did.

BLACK FRATERNITIES ARE TOO WILD

During the spring of 1974, which was my junior year, another issue of race came up. Prior to that semester, the University of Alabama had never allowed any African American Greek organizations to have a presence on campus.

But that year, the powers that be made the announcement that they would begin allowing Black fraternities and sororities to operate on campus. Most football players did not join fraternities. Out of 125 players on the team, we might have had 8-10 who were in fraternities at any given time.

However, I was immediately drawn to the opportunity. One of the neighbors I grew up with in my community had been a member of Omega Psi Phi. He wore the colors very well, and had represented with honor what it meant to be a member of this organization. They stood for community outreach, charity work, a strong work ethic, and good character. Besides that, the men of Omega Psi Phi put a premium on education and academics.

Having such a positive impression of the organization, I had always had an interest in joining. My brother Theron had also joined a fraternity after being influenced by our neighbor, but it had not been an option for me at Alabama.

Once the officials at Alabama gave us the green light, there were still obstacles to be overcome. Because there were no existing chapters to pledge, we had to get people from other campuses to come to the UA campus so that we could pledge according to the rules of the organizations.

We found a solution in the existing chapters at Stillman College, a historically Black college located in Tuscaloosa, just a short drive from the UA campus. But for me, there was yet another obstacle—one that was potentially much bigger and more difficult to overcome.

As a football player, I had to run everything by my coaches. Given that there were always 8-10 white players in fraternities at any given time, I did not expect any considerable pushback on my decision to pledge.

I was wrong.

Almost immediately, my coaches tried to slam the door

shut on me joining. In their minds, the white fraternities on campus were well-established. They knew what to expect. But they did not know what to expect from Black fraternities. Adding to the trouble, they said that they had heard a good bit about Black fraternities—that they were wild party organizations and not much more.

Their other big concern was that it would take up too much of my time. So once again, I think this was an area where prejudices and biases were lingering. It was important for someone to challenge those biases. I felt strongly that they were wrong about Black fraternities.

My impression of Black fraternities, based on the people I had met personally, was quite the opposite. Yes, they had social events and parties, but they were very much focused on God, academics, charity work, community involvement, and character building.

As best I can recall, that initial meeting with my coaches went something like this.

The coaches: "You don't need to be part of that. You're already part of a football team. Fraternities are where you go to identify with others and become part of a family, but you already have a family in your football team. The other part of it is that we hear they're pretty rowdy. They party all the time, and you don't need that—we don't need that as part of our football family. So we don't think this is a good idea, and we're going to have to say no."

Just as I had done with the issue of going to business school, I could not accept their answer. Something in me just led me to persevere in these types of situations. As I recall, I never brought up the fact that white players were already joining fraternities at will. Instead, I just did my best to state my case and help them see where they were getting it wrong on this issue.

> **Me:** "Well, with all due respect, I think this is very important and worthy of further consideration. Every historically Black college and university has Greek organizations. They're national organizations, so they're well-established and they have good reputations. They do a lot of really positive things. Yes, they may have hazing issues from time to time just like any other fraternity. I'm sure they throw parties. But that's not what they're all about. They do a lot of good for the community, and a lot of their members go on to be successful in life because the organization builds character and teaches them how to be successful."

> **The coaches:** "Eh . . . it's just a place to party, Ralph. Come on . . . that's all it is, and we say no."

I continued to state my case, probably in a somewhat repetitive fashion, and they continued to repeat their answer. It was a solid no.

I did not accept that answer.

In frustration, that led them to refer me to Coach Bryant, just as they had with the business school decision.

> **The coaches:** "Look, Ralph. Our answer is no, so if you want to pursue this any further, you're going to have to go see Coach Bryant."

After doing a little research, I promptly called Coach

Bryant's assistant and asked her if I could have an appointment to see the Coach. I would pretty much be standing alone on this issue. It's not that everyone saw me fighting some kind of civil rights battle and didn't want to join me, but most of the other athletes just weren't interested in joining a fraternity.

None of the basketball players wanted to go through a pledge process. I couldn't get any of my football teammates interested either. I'd be going to Coach Bryant's office alone.

The day of the meeting, I went in and Coach Bryant said, "Ralph, I understand you're interested in joining a fraternity. I'd like to know three things. Why do you want to do it? What value will it add? What distractions will it cause for you?"

"Well coach, Black fraternities do a lot of very good things. They help shape Black men through character building, and they provide a family to connect with. Yes, our football team does that as well, but the fraternity provides a national organization to identify with after college. There are chapters for this fraternity all over the country, and they enjoy a very good reputation. Football gives me a local family while I'm here at school, but the fraternity will give me a national family that will be there for me everywhere I go. And they do so many positive things in terms of staying focused on God, on the community, on helping others, and just being good citizens. So I'd really like to be a part of that."

As best I can recall, Coach Bryant never mentioned anything about "Black" fraternities, their reputation, or anything to do with race. As always, he was concerned about me succeeding as a person. He responded, "Ralph, my biggest concern is that you stay on top of your classwork while also fulfilling all of your obligations to the team. You know what that means. Practice. Training. Meetings. Making all of your classes and assignments. Can you do all of that while also pledging the fraternity?"

"Coach, there are hundreds of players in the NFL right now who successfully navigated classwork, football, and fraternity life. Yes, it can be done, and yes, I can do it. I don't see any reason why I can't do it and still maintain everything else."

At that point, Coach Bryant continued to ask me questions, and it was clear he had already done some of his own research. Overall, he appeared to believe that this would be a positive thing, but he expressed continued concern. He did not want anything to interfere with my academics or my football, but he summarized his thoughts by saying, "Ralph, it sounds like this is going to be a good thing, so I'm going to let you go ahead. But we will, of course, monitor your academics and your football, and if anything starts slipping, this will have to go."

Once Coach Bryant gave me approval to join a fraternity, a couple of the other Black players decided to pledge as well. One of them tried it for a short time and stopped, but John Mitchell and I moved ahead. We joined the newly established Omega Psi Phi Inc., Beta Eta Chapter, becoming charter members.

As it turns out, pledging the fraternity was a good bit of extra work but it was also a great decision for me. Theron and I are both members, along with hundreds of thousands of other African American men across the country. There are chapters now which have Caucasian men as well. All in all, it's a unique brotherhood and I would encourage any young man who has the opportunity, to seriously consider pledging.

As I reflect on the experience of seeking to join a fraternity at UA, I think it's worth noting that whenever I was referred to Coach Bryant on an issue that involved prejudice or discrimination, he always seemed to be in my corner. He never voiced a prejudicial opinion to me, but instead seemed to view every situation in light of how it would affect me as a person. If something was going to be good for me and contribute to my success in life, Coach Bryant was all for it. If something was not going to be good for me, he wasn't going to allow it.

As best I can tell, he was always looking out for the best interest of his players—especially me.

COACH BRYANT OWNS HIS MISTAKE

While there were probably many examples, one more story stands out in my mind as illustrating that Coach Bryant was serious about looking out for my best interests, and that he was very serious about honoring his word.

One day during my sophomore year, I was walking out of Bryant Hall after a nice lunch. I guess I was looking to the side but continuing to walk forward because I almost walked all the way into Coach Bryant. He stopped me, put his hand on my shoulder, and said, "Ralph, I am very disappointed in you. Very disappointed. And to that point, I called your mom this morning to talk to her about it."

I was almost in a panic—at least internally. While trying to show no emotion, my mind was racing with all the things he could have been talking about. What had I done that he had found out about? What could I have possibly done that warranted a call to my mother? Why is Coach Bryant so disappointed in me?

I could not figure it out.

He continued, "But your mother and I talked about it. And I made a commitment to her that this will not happen again."

"Okay . . . "

I guess he could tell that I still hadn't figured out what this was about.

"I got your grades yesterday, Ralph. You did pretty well, overall. But you got a C in your major. There is no reason for you to get a C in your major. That means you didn't pay attention. That means you didn't try. You weren't working hard enough, and that's on me. I should have made sure you were working hard on your classwork. But I won't make that mistake again. I promised your mother that I won't. This will not happen again."

I had no idea he was watching my grades that closely. I had not seen *any* of my grades yet, but he had seen all of them! From that point on, I did concentrate on my schoolwork more closely—especially in my major. That external pressure helped give me the extra motivation I needed.

But what was significant about that moment was that Coach Bryant was making good on his promises. One of the reasons he was watching my grades so closely was that during his recruiting visit to our home, he had promised my mom that he would "be my father away from home" and that he would "take care of me." He meant that, and he followed through on his word.

And when he felt like he had failed in that commitment, even in the slightest way, it genuinely bothered him. He sought immediately to correct *his* mistake.

Not everyone in life operates that way. If you find a

mentor or leader who genuinely cares about your success, you should listen to, appreciate, and value that person. Learn from them and let them develop you. Don't listen to any other voices that tell you to distrust a person or hold bitterness toward them because of their race or even their past sins.

Human beings make mistakes. But they also correct their mistakes. And we do ourselves a disservice when we refuse to forgive people. If I had shunned Coach Bryant's leadership because of his past mistakes, it would not have hurt him. I would have only hurt myself.

Every year—even after I graduated—Coach Bryant sent flowers and a personal note to my mother on her birthday. They both shared the same birthday, which was September 11th.

The man honored my mother and his commitment to her in many ways. He even went beyond his commitment to take care of me while I was at Alabama. When the time was getting close for me to graduate, Coach Bryant called me, Robert Fraley, and Ricky Davis into his office.

Over the years, Ricky's dad had encouraged and influenced us. Wanting to see us have the best future we could have, he had gotten all of us seriously considering law school. In fact, for a time, I had planned to go to law school, and Coach Bryant knew of that plan. He also knew that law school was very expensive.

Coach Bryant got right to the point and offered to pay for all three of us to go to law school. I don't know if he was planning to set up a scholarship or exactly how that would work, but that was his offer: "If you boys will go to law school at Alabama, I will pay for it."

By that time, I had already decided against law school. I'd

had enough of the books and was ready to go out and apply what I had learned. So I politely declined Coach Bryant's offer. Ricky headed to the NFL. Robert already had plans to go to Georgetown Law School, so none of us took him up on the offer, at least not at that time. Robert ultimately went to law school at Alabama, so he may have come back and accepted the offer. I don't know for sure.

But what's so interesting about Coach Bryant's offer is that there was no benefit to him. We were done at Alabama. We didn't have any more eligibility to play football. I feel certain that his primary motivation was to make sure we all had the best future we could possibly have. He genuinely wanted what was best for his players.

Most of the time, when people talk about Coach Bryant, they talk about what a great coach he was. He did win more games than any other college football coach in history, and that record stood for many years. So of course, people still talk about that.

They talk about the 6 national championships. That he had a brilliant football mind. He made great in-game adjustments, and he outcoached just about everybody. He was also an excellent recruiter.

All of that is absolutely true. I have a great deal of respect for Paul Bryant, the coach. But I go beyond that and honor the greatness of the man. He was a man of character who taught me a lot and helped me in many ways. He was incredibly focused on making us the best we could be on and off the field.

Coach Bryant challenged us to be our best in the classroom, and in our character, just as much as he challenged us on the football field. He often challenged us to be the "best neighbors" and the "best citizens" we could be.

He pushed us to pursue excellence in the dorm as much as in the practice facility. And if a man wasn't performing up to his standard, that man would face Coach Bryant's wrath. And he'd be made better for it.

I know I was.

When I sum up everything I know about Coach Bryant, I would have to say that I respect the character of the man just as much as—and maybe even more than—the greatness of the coach.

9

THE INSURANCE INDUSTRY: DESPERATELY SEEKING INTEGRATION

Going back to the time of my recruitment at Alabama, I had a wonderful mentor named T. Raymond Perdue. Raymond was a successful white businessman and booster for the Alabama football team. He was an extremely nice man who treated me very well. He taught me many things about the fundamentals of the business world, business etiquette, and so forth.

Raymond genuinely took an interest in me and wanted to see me do well in life. If you ever find someone like that, be sure to value and appreciate that person and the relationship you have with them.

When I graduated, I did not have a clear path of where I wanted to go. For a long time, law school was the plan. But I had decided against law school without having a new plan in place. My major was Marketing and my minor was Economics.

I understood money flow and sales.

Interviewing with big companies like Procter & Gamble, I had gotten several job offers but was still undecided. Then one day Raymond calls me up and says, "I've got a job for you. I want you to go to work for a company I've represented—Provident Life and Accident. You'll be selling insurance."

"No thanks, I don't want to do that," was my immediate reply.

The only insurance agent I had ever seen in my life was a debit agent who came door to door in the Black communities to collect life insurance premiums. Most of the people I was around growing up had $2,000 or $5,000 life insurance policies.

The debit agent had a little book, and he would come around once every two weeks or once a month. You'd give him $2, and he would mark it down in his debit book, keeping your policy in effect. That was my concept of insurance sales.

"I'm not going door to door picking up $2 for people's life insurance policies," I told Raymond resolutely.

"No, it's not that kind of insurance. You'll be selling insurance contracts to large companies. When they contract with you, you'll be getting paid part of the premium on thousands of medical, dental, vision, and life insurance policies. You'll be selling the contracts through brokers and consultants. You'll work directly with those brokers and consultants, so you won't be going door to door selling anything."

"Okay. I've never heard of that." I still wasn't quite sure what to think.

"Trust me. It's the right thing for you to do. They'll give you a company car. They'll give you an expense account. You get to go entertain people, and do fun stuff and make good money. It's a great job!"

"Raymond, I've never heard of any of this. I just have no idea what you're talking about."

"I know you don't, but trust me. You've trusted me all these years. Trust me on this." Raymond's response was convincing. He'd spent almost 5 years showing me that he had my best interest in mind. He clearly knew what he was talking about. I could trust him.

Provident had been extremely successful at getting contracts for textile mills and other large employers, but they had never had a Black sales representative. Not a single one. This was a very large, nationwide insurance company. It was 1975, and they had never had a Black sales rep anywhere in the country.

They were looking to change that. I don't know the details of how that decision came about, but their wanting to hire me was not an accident. Raymond told them I was a Black football player with a marketing degree and that I would do great. They agreed to hire me before they'd ever even met me, much less interviewed me.

You often hear in life that "It's not just what you know, it's who you know." That may sound on the surface like the same thing as saying, "Well, you have to be lucky." But knowing people doesn't happen by accident any more than knowing things. I'd spent 5 years showing Raymond that I was humble and hungry. I was respectful, and I had a good attitude. He knew I wasn't going to let him down or embarrass him in any way.

We had developed a relationship of trust. He was comfortable giving me his highest recommendation because we had built up personal equity with each other.

Of course, I still had to go through the interview process, even though it was a given that I was hired. It's unlikely that you will ever get a job for a large company without going through the interview process, even if you're the CEO's son. That's just how it works even if the process is merely a formality.

But even if you feel like you have it in the bag, go above and beyond anyway. Really prepare. Arrive early. Ask good questions. Be engaged. Take notes. Follow up. Don't give them even the slightest sense that you believe you've got it in the bag, even if they are practically insisting that you do.

That's a really good way to impress some people.

After going through the interviews and basically getting an offer, they still had to find a specific office for me to work out of. They have offices with sales agents all around the country. With me being the first ever African American to do this, they wanted to be strategic about where they placed me.

The obvious place would have been Birmingham, Alabama. Most of the businesspeople in that area knew who I was. I had been a high school star, a highly publicized recruit at Alabama, and a contributing member of the 1973 National Championship team. It probably seemed like a no brainer.

But the head of the Birmingham office flat refused. He just said it would not fly around Alabama. He didn't believe there was any way the people in Alabama would buy insurance from me. My status as a reasonably well-known athlete was not enough to persuade him.

He stated firmly, "No matter if he was the biggest sports star in the world, white people in Alabama will not do business with Black people."

Corporate's next idea was the Memphis office. Corporate called and talked to the head of the Memphis office about the possibility of me working there. Same response.

"Oh, no. That will not happen in Memphis. People in Memphis won't do business with him."

Knoxville office. Same response. "Nope, can't bring him here."

This continued with offices all around the country.

Corporate had committed to hire me, but it was starting to look like there was not going to be anywhere for me to work. No office would accept me, all on the premise that I wouldn't be successful there because of my race.

Finally, they found a man who was willing to take me on: J. Marshall Dye, in Greenville, South Carolina. Greenville was actually one of the largest, most successful offices for Provident at that time because South Carolina had a huge textile industry.

GOADED INTO INTEGRATION

Marshall Dye had grown up in Mississippi, and he had been around the KKK all his life. Some of his family members had been Klansmen. He never told me that he had been in the Klan himself, but he obviously had spent a lot of time around the Klan and had a lot of personal connections to its members.

Marshall had gone to college at Ole Miss and he loved the Confederate flag—or the "rebel flag" as it was usually referred to in those days. He was a WWII veteran, and a very headstrong man.

So Foy Watson, an executive at the corporate office, called him up and basically said, "Hey, we've got this Black guy up here that we think is going to be a star in the insurance world. We really wanted to send him to you because you're the best trainer and teacher we've got. And he'd be a great asset to you, because he's gonna be good.

"But we know we can't send him to you because your brokers would never let you have a Black man working in your office. Your business partners and your customers would never allow it either. I mean—let's face it, they have the final say, and they'd never let you have a Black person in your office."

It was the classic reverse psychology play, and it worked like a charm.

"The hell they won't! Nobody controls me! They can't tell me what to do. You send him over here right now." Marshall was indignant, and corporate was ecstatic.

FIRST DAY ON THE JOB: DON'T KILL THE WHITE MAN

As a young man, I had the attitude that I was bulletproof. I'd pretty much never been scared of anything in my life. And even though Raymond and the business school had tried to instill some professional etiquette into me, I was still somewhat unpolished.

Growing up around my dad, I had been exposed to plenty of business activity. There was a lot of useful knowledge, but everyone was working class. I just didn't grow up around doctors, attorneys, bankers, and other sophisticated professional types.

So when I showed up for my first day on the job, I had on a blue suit with white trim and piping around the jacket. My shoes had 3-inch platform heels. And I had a 4-inch afro.

It was a great look for a college campus in 1975. But in a business setting, it just wasn't the right look.

If that wasn't enough, I had a toothpick in the side of my mouth, because I'd just come from breakfast with one of the other sales agents. I strolled into Marshall Dye's office to meet him for the first time.

When I walked in, he promptly stood up and began walking toward me. Assuming that was for a handshake, I remained relaxed and undisturbed. That is, until he got a little closer and opened his mouth.

"What the hell are you doing?" he demanded.

His question was promptly followed by a slap right to the side of my face. He had been moving to snatch the toothpick out of my mouth, so it was really kind of a combination snatch and slap. He hit and grabbed at the same time.

Now, I had just come off of the football field—a tough place with a lot of tough guys. Guys who weren't used to putting up with any garbage from anyone. And I definitely had that kind of attitude. To be honest, I was a little bit crazy when it came to that kind of thing.

It took everything in me to keep from busting this man's head wide open.

I remember saying internally to myself, "Ralph, don't you hit this white man. If you hit this white man and kill him your first day on the job, you're not going to have a long career. Don't you hit this man."

I don't know if this was a race issue or not. Marshall had been an officer in the Navy, and he was generally as mean as three snakes. He had probably caught a few snatch-slaps of his own over the years. Things were different back then when it comes to physical expression among men.

For example, if a coach grabs or shoves a player now, it's a huge scandal. If a coach or other authority figure grabbed a player or smacked them back in those days, it wasn't exactly normal, but it wasn't a huge scandal either.

Marshall followed up his slap by barking at me. "Son, don't you ever walk into my office with a stick in your mouth like that. And don't you ever come in here with those high heel shoes on. You will dress appropriately for the job, understand?"

He hadn't said, "Good morning."

"Nice to meet you."

There was none of that. We had never met before, and this was how our relationship was starting?

Very calmly, and very firmly, I replied, "Yes, sir. I won't. And don't *you* ever—*ever* put your hand on me like that again."

He didn't say anything back. We just stood there and stared each other down for what seemed like a very long time. After a while, he just started barking orders again as he would with any new rep.

"Go out there and get your paperwork done, then I've got two books you need to read. We'll go over them and there will be a test at the end of the week."

This was new territory for both of us. Not only had Marshall never had a Black sales representative, Marshall had never dealt with a Black person in any professional setting at all.

It would have been very easy for me to turn around that day and walk out. It probably would have been even easier for me to take out my anger by beating this man down. Only in his late 40s at the time, Marshall was a tough older man to be sure. But I had him when it came to youth, size, and strength. I could have satisfied that desire we all feel in those kinds of situations, and it would have felt good in that moment.

But I'm really glad I didn't do that.

Our first couple of weeks continued to be pretty rough. Marshall and I bumped heads pretty regularly. He was hard-nosed and hardheaded. I was hardheaded. I wasn't scared of anyone, and I didn't back down from anyone.

He didn't either, and we were both half-crazy in that way. But it wasn't long before we began to respect each other. I began to see that Marshall was truly trying to help me, and Marshall began to see that I was genuinely interested in learning and growing.

It wasn't too long before Marshall had taught me to be successful in the insurance business, and I owe a lot of my success to him. In probably one of the strangest and funniest stories of my life, I also owe him credit for my marriage.

10

GOD BRINGS THE RIGHT PEOPLE INTO OUR LIVES

During my junior year at Alabama, I dated a girl that I would pick up at Martha Parham Hall—the women's dormitory where she lived. Every time I went to pick her up for a date, she was late.

I think she must have wanted to keep me waiting, but she wasn't just a little bit late. She was very late, usually a half hour or so.

I probably would have been upset about it except for this one thing. There was this really cute girl named Debra who worked at the reception desk in the lobby. So I would just hang out and talk to Debra every time I was waiting for this other girl.

After a month or so, Debra and I realized that we were really hitting it off. She dropped her boyfriend. I dropped the other girl, and we just started going out together.

I guess the moral of that story is don't be late, because you might miss out. I'm kidding. I'm sure the other young lady went on to have a wonderful life.

Anyway, after we had been on a few dates, I told Debra, "I won't be able to see you very much starting next week."

"What? Why not?" she asked, concerned.

"Because I have to start spring practice," I responded, stating what I considered to be "the obvious."

"Spring practice for *what*? What does that mean?" She seemed surprised and concerned. And confused.

"What? You don't know who I am?!" My ego was bruised. But after I licked my wounds, I realized I'd just won the dating jackpot. She had no idea I played football. She didn't know the first thing about football, nor did she care about it at all. She'd never been to a football game in her life.

She only liked me for me.

AN ARRANGED MARRIAGE

Debra and I dated during most of my junior and senior years of college, but Debra was a year behind me in school. A couple of months after I began working for Marshall, I was in North Carolina for some business meetings and sales calls. One of my colleagues, Mike, was mentoring me. In between sales visits, we stopped in and called the home office in Greenville.

"You've got to get back right away!" the voice on the other end of the line stated with some urgency. It was Marshall, and he wasn't joking.

Mike said, "No, we can't do that. We have more sales calls to do."

"No, you've got to come back right now," Marshall explained.

"Why? We've got so much more to do," Mike protested.

"Mike, I'm telling you—you and Ralph get back to

Greenville right now." Marshall wasn't making a suggestion. This former Naval Officer was issuing a direct order.

So we made the roughly two hour drive back to Greenville, walked in the door, and asked Marshall, "Okay, what's wrong?"

"Oh, nothing. Nothing's wrong. Mike, go do your job. Ralph, you've had a tough day. You need to go home."

We had no idea what to make of his strange directives. Marshall was a business first kind of guy. It didn't make any sense that he would call us back home in the middle of sales visits and send me home in the middle of the day just because he thought I needed a little break.

"Okay . . . um, I don't need to go home. I need to work," I responded in a confused tone.

"No! Go home!" Marshall retorted.

So I went home to my apartment, and to my very pleasant surprise, I found Debra there waiting on me.

As it turned out, she had come to surprise me with a visit. But since she didn't have a way to get into my apartment, and she didn't know anyone else in Greenville, she had gone to my office.

With me being away, she began to meet the people in my office. They brought her in to see Marshall, and he thought she was just the sweetest thing in the world. He had bought her lunch and then arranged for the manager of my apartment complex to let her into my apartment.

Debra was really excited to have met Marshall.

"He is such a nice man!" She went on and on about how wonderful and accommodating Marshall had been to her.

Debra ended up staying for several days, maybe even a whole week. It was nice being together, but she still had not finished her degree at UA. At the end of our weeklong visit, I said, "Okay, Debra, I've loved having you, but you have to go back to school."

"No, I've decided I'm not going back to school. I'm staying here with you," she announced.

"Uh . . . well, no. You can't do that. You can't stay here with me. You have to go back and finish school." She had really caught me off guard.

"No, I'm not going back to school," she persisted.

I thought, "Okay, we've got a little dilemma here . . . "

When Marshall heard about this latest development, he kept telling me, "This is the greatest girl in the world. You're crazy if you don't marry this girl."

Another three weeks or so passed and Debra was still there.

Marshall knew she was still there, so he called me into his office one day.

"Okay, so what's the plan?" he inquired.

"What do you mean? What plan?" I assumed his question was in reference to something business related.

"What's the plan about Debra? What are you gonna do?"

"I—I don't know. I don't really have a plan." It was true. I didn't have a plan.

But Marshall did.

"Here's the plan. I've already talked to my friend, Jim, who's a judge down at the county courthouse. We have an appointment tomorrow at noon for you to get married. Jim has already got you on his calendar."

"Marshall! I can't get married!" I stated emphatically. Had this man lost his mind? What was he talking about? He had been trying to persuade me to marry Debra, just making comments here and there. But I had no immediate plans to get married.

I continued, "We haven't taken a blood test." I was desperately searching for an excuse that would end the conversation.

"In South Carolina, you don't have to have a blood test," Marshall responded, shooting down the best excuse I could muster at the time. He continued, "You don't have to have a witness either. You just need a judge, and I've got you one. It's all taken care of. Tomorrow at noon. Be there. And by the way, you have to give the judge a tip. So be sure to give him a nice tip."

That was it. The discussion was over. That night, Debra got out a dress that she really wanted to wear.

We got married the next day at noon, and I gave the judge $20 as a tip.

That was 45 years ago. We've gone through plenty of ups and downs over the years, but our marriage has been great, allowing us to build a family of two daughters. Our oldest, Deidre Jur-l Stokes, is a UNC Chapel Hill grad and a Howard School of Law attorney practicing in the metro Atlanta area. Rashele Antoinette is our youngest daughter. She is an 11 year marketing representative with a national research company. Rashele and her husband, Richard Eric Bradshaw, are the proud parents of our two beautiful granddaughters, Parker Elise, and Layna Elizabeth.

Debra is a wonderful wife, and I owe a huge debt of gratitude to Marshall Dye for having "arranged" my marriage.

Marshall was extremely good to us over the years in many ways. For years, Debra and I would have dinner at Marshall's house once a week. Marshall and his wife, Barbara, became our parents away from home. His two children were a joy to know. Years later, Marshall's daughter worked for me out of my insurance office, and we all continue to share a connection.

Debra and I came to understand later on that Marshall's urging us to get married came out of his genuine desire to see the best for his employees. As Debra tells it, Marshall was a lot like Coach Bryant. He cared about his business, but he also cared just as much about the people who worked for him. He treated them like family.

It was a family business for him, and if you worked for him, you were in the family. There was no separating family and business for Marshall. It was all wrapped up together.

A short time after Debra moved to Greenville, she applied for a store credit card. She had not gotten a job yet, so when the application asked for job and income, she put down my job. And then she put down *her best guess* for my income.

I had never mentioned how much money I was making, so she just put down what seemed reasonable for her in 1975 —$450 per month. They called Provident to verify my salary, and Marshall got wind that Debra had put it down to be $450 per month.

He called Debra and said, "How dare you make it look like I don't pay my people well?"

She defended herself by explaining that she really had no idea what I made. But Marshall was upset. He was highly insulted because taking good care of his people—his extended family—was that important to him. He prided himself on it.

MARSHALL DYE'S LASTING LEGACY

When I first took the job with Marshall and rented an apartment, it came with a house plant. That plant is still alive to this day, 46 years later. We've moved all over the country during the years since we first met Marshall. That plant was probably in the garage at some point. It has been left outside. It was thrown around and put in storage at other times, but somehow that plant has survived and made it through every move.

I like to think that plant is symbolic of Marshall's influence on my life. I keep it in my home office to this day as a reminder of my relationship with him.

In March of 2020, J. Marshall Dye II passed on from this life at the age of 92. I was honored to give the primary tribute at his funeral. He was truly one of a kind, and a tremendous human being.

We had a rocky start those first couple of weeks. But Marshall and I were a match made in Heaven. He ended up being my personal and professional mentor. This man from Mississippi taught me business in ways I'd never learned it before. He taught me how to be successful.

He even taught me ways of thinking that I'd never learned anywhere else. Apart from my wife and children, he was the best thing that ever happened to me.

Keep in mind, this was a man who had grown up around the KKK. If you had set us down and given us various options, this is probably not a man I would have chosen to work for. And he probably wouldn't have chosen to hire me as his first choice. But God has a way of bringing the right people into your life, at just the right time, for reasons only He understands at the time.

Some time after we had met, gotten to know each other, and worked closely together, Marshall had a confession to make.

He said, "Ralph, you are the first Black professional I've

ever known or had any interaction with. You know what's so strange, my parents always told me growing up that Black people are ignorant. They're not intelligent. They can't speak properly—that Black people are just not very smart."

He continued, "My parents also told me that the stove was hot. And if I went over there and put my hand on that stove, I found that they were right. It was hot. My parents told me Black people were not as smart as white people. Why wouldn't I believe them? Everything else they told me proved true. So, in my mind, why would they lie to me about this?

"Until you came along, I guess I still believed that deep down. I just never really felt the need to question that belief before. But you push back. You challenge me in ways I've never been challenged. You go and ace every examination and get every credential the insurance industry has to offer. What I'm trying to say is, I know now that my parents were wrong."

Marshall Dye was a magnificent human being—and one that like so many others in my life, I could have simply written off as a racist after our initial experiences together. I could have decided to hate him or be bitter toward him. Or I could watch him grow and prosper and become a better person in an area where *he* needed *my* help.

That was the choice set before me, and I know I made the right one.

11

BLACK IS NOT A LIABILITY

When I went to work for Provident, I knew I was their first ever Black sales representative. Later on, I found out that none of our competitors had one either. For many years, I was the first and only Black sales representative in the Southeast region when it came to health and life insurance contract sales for large companies. As you can imagine, I stood out from the crowd anytime I was in a business meeting.

NO EXCUSES

Very early in my career, I had to go sell insurance to a guy who was known to be a racist. He was the president of a large organization, and my company was in the running to get a large insurance contract from them.

This particular meeting, I was accompanied by only one colleague—a young white man named Tom, who had been on the job for about two weeks. Tom was not incompetent, of course, but he didn't have any idea what he was doing. He was brand new and completely inexperienced.

When we went into the meeting, the racist executive made it very clear that he had no interest in speaking with me. He did not shake my hand. He did not acknowledge me. He directed all of his statements and questions to Tom.

Every time, Tom would respond by indicating that he didn't know the answer, and he would defer to me. But there was a problem. I didn't know some of the answers either.

We did not get the contract.

When we got back, my boss said, "It's okay. I knew you weren't going to sell this guy because he's a racist and he didn't want to buy from you."

My immediate response was, "No. That's not why I didn't get the contract. He may or may not have been a racist—He probably was. But that's not why I didn't get the contract. I didn't get the contract because I wasn't prepared. And that's not ever going to happen again."

I meant it.

The reality is that I had not properly studied up before this meeting. I had failed to anticipate their questions. Poor preparation makes for poor execution. Racist president or not, I believe I could have gotten that contract if I had properly prepared for the meeting.

And until I had properly prepared and executed to the best of my ability, there was no point in blaming anyone else for the result. Judging why another person made their decision wasn't going to help me. Blaming them wasn't going to help me. But looking at my own performance and recognizing where I needed improvement—now that was going to help me tremendously.

The truth is that my presentation was so poor, my own

mother wouldn't have bought from me that day. And I had to own that.

Making excuses and having a poor attitude are one of the most common ways people limit how far they will go in life. If a racist person can get you blaming *their* racism for the results *you* get in life, you've basically let them win. You've given them power over you—and it's power that they don't really have unless you give it to them.

So the answer is to make sure you don't give them that power.

As I write this, Heisman Trophy winner Devonta Smith just finished his senior season at Alabama and is being evaluated by NFL scouts. Devonta is listed at 6' 1" and 175 pounds. Some people question the accuracy of that height measurement, which is often the case for smaller players. Either way, you can look at Devonta and tell that he has a small frame. He also looks very thin.

Many people question whether he can truly make it at the next level. Can he handle the physical rigor?

There's just one issue with their skepticism. When Devonta was in high school, people questioned whether he could make it in college because of his size. During his underclassmen years in high school, he was often teased about his weight—at that time only 140 pounds.[1] The size issue has always followed him in his football career.

But if you read about Devonta Smith a little more, you'll learn that he always stays after practice and catches 100 extra passes. After all the hard work is done and everyone is exhausted, he stays behind and keeps working. And he has done that going all the way back to junior high.

No matter how hard he worked, and how much he achieved, people always seem determined to discount him because of the one thing he can't do much to change: his size.

But he just keeps on working hard. He keeps on achieving. So far, he keeps showing everyone that he's one of the best football players in the country, and possibly one of the best ever to play the game. He broke all kinds of receiving records in college, and was the first wide receiver to win the Heisman Trophy in 29 years. During his senior season, he dropped only two passes all year.

His on-field results are absolutely astounding.

Can you imagine if he had believed his critics? What if he had let their opinion of him shape his future? That wouldn't have been to his benefit at all. He couldn't do much about his size, so he focused on the things he could control.

We cannot ultimately control whether other people have racist attitudes or not. But we can control our own response to people and to situations we face in life. When our focus is on the things we can control, we have a much better chance of rising above the noise. The criticism. The injustice.

Don't ever let being Black become a liability in your mind. Refuse to take on a victim mentality. Being Black, or any minority, gives a person a unique perspective and unique opportunities to make an impact in this world. In many ways, being Black gives a person greater opportunity to influence others.

Being Black is an advantage and an asset, but we must choose to view it that way.

"If you search for good, you will find favor; but if you search for evil, it will find you!"

— PROVERBS 11:27 NLT

HARD WORK BUILDS A CAREER

When I first got hired with Provident, it was partly because I knew Raymond Perdue. For some reason, he convinced them they should hire me, and he sold them on the idea of having a Black sales representative.

Years later, in the 1980s, I was a senior sales representative in Chattanooga. Provident had hundreds of sales agents in offices all across the country. In spite of the Chattanooga market's limited size, I finished in the top 10 nationally every year for sales, and most of the time I was in the top 5.

I loved Chattanooga. This is where both of our daughters, Deidre and Rashele, were born so it had a special place in our hearts. I had gotten extremely well plugged in to the community, and that meant tons of repeat business. It got to the point that I could generate a six-figure income there in my sleep.

One morning in my early 30s, I woke up with this thought in my mind, "Wow. I could live in Chattanooga for the rest of my life. I love it here. I love all the people, and they love me. It's so easy for me here. I am successful, and I can continue to be successful here with almost no effort."

Right after I had that thought, something clicked.

That exact same morning, when I arrived at work, I spoke to the Senior Vice President in charge of our office. "Foy, I have got to leave here. I've got to get out of this city. I'll be leaving at some point within the next 6 months."

When you wake up and decide you can stay in a particular situation because it's so easy, you're in trouble. At least that was how I saw it at the time, and it proved correct.

In general, you don't walk away from things in life that are going really well.

But there was no more challenge for me in Chattanooga. I could have stayed on easy street there, and that just wouldn't have been healthy for me as a person. I believe I would have set myself up for personal and probably even professional failure by staying in a situation that held no challenge for me.

Later, I became the Regional Director with Provident over the Florida, Georgia, Alabama, and Puerto Rico region. After that, I took a job with Cigna Healthcare. At Cigna, I was a Vice President and then a Senior Vice President. It was an executive, corner-office position, and again, I was blessed with tremendous success.

While I may have gotten the initial hire at Provident by knowing Raymond, I got everything else by working my tail off, selling a ton of insurance, and developing strong management skills. I pursued and obtained every type of credential the insurance industry had to offer, including the CLU, FLMI, MHP, and HIA. The big key to my success was my commitment to learn everything I could about how to be successful, to implement that knowledge, and then to lead others in doing the same.

None of it came by accident.

If you see any person at the top—especially a Black person—you can bet they didn't get there without a ton of hard work and sacrifice.

12

DOING THE THINGS BLACK PEOPLE CAN'T DO

Several times now, I've mentioned that I believe God had a calling on my life for the cause of integration, going all the way back to my time at Robert E. Lee High School. For most of my life, that calling has manifested through me having an impact on white people much more than Black people.

While I fully supported all things related to civil rights, I've never personally given any rousing civil rights speeches. I've never organized any rallies. When the opportunity presents itself, of course, I have always tried to impact young Black people. One of the primary ways I've done that was by breaking barriers.

But I really believe one of the most profound impacts I had was by doing all the things that "Black people can't do." Having been born in 1953, I grew up during a time when most people in white society believed the following:

- *Black people cannot speak the king's English.*
- *Black people cannot make a subject and verb agree.*

- *Black people cannot sit down at a dinner table and use the right utensils or display proper manners.*
- *Black people can't hold an intelligent conversation.*
- *Black people cannot lead white people. If there are white people in a business, they have to lead and the Black people have to follow.*

In most white people's minds, Black people were relegated to certain roles—basically a second-class citizen kind of status—mostly fueled by false beliefs about what Black people could or could not do.

That bothered me.

My response was to live my life in such a way that those notions would be proven false. I resolved that when people looked at me, they would see a person who was respectful. Professional. Ethical. Prepared. Responsible. Capable. Polite. Friendly.

My resolve was that people would always see this Black man doing things the right way. The goal, initially, was to allow them to see "a Black man doing it right." But after a while, when you've done it right long enough, they stop seeing a Black man doing it right, and then just start to see a person doing it right.

You can be the guy on social media who shows everyone how resentful he is toward a huge portion of the population. Or you can be the guy who proves racism wrong by having a great attitude and pursuing excellence in everything you do. It's much more healthy for our society when we take the latter approach. It's also a lot more personally advantageous. These next two stories illustrate that principle quite well.

SELLING INSURANCE TO THE KKK

During my time in Chattanooga, we had received a request for proposal from a large company in Tullahoma, Tennessee. This was the early 80s, so things were still very different than they are now.

When the request came in, my superiors at Provident told me, "You can't do this presentation because the president of the company is the KKK imperial wizard for middle Tennessee. You need to let Bill do it by himself."

My response was simple, "It's my sale. My case. It came in through my broker. So if we sell the case, who gets paid?"

"You get paid."

"No, I don't get paid for work I don't do. So I'll be doing the presentation myself." That was my final answer.

Bill and I drove to Tullahoma and we met with three people there. The broker, the president of the company, and the benefit director for the company. When I walked in, everyone shook my hand—everyone except the company president.

But his disdain didn't stop there. He wouldn't even look at me.

We all sat down at a big boardroom table. The broker, the benefit director, and the president sat on one side. Bill and I sat on the other side.

By this point in my career, I had learned some key things about sales presentations. First, preparation is a major key to success. The request for proposal gave us a lot of information and insight into a potential client's needs and preferences. Generally, the client will outline why they're going to market.

Maybe they are just shopping for a lower price. It could

be that there are certain benefits they want, but could not obtain from their current provider. Sometimes clients would be unhappy with the administration and service of their current provider. Other times, it was all of the above.

But even if it was all of the above, typically you could study the RFP and get a sense of which items were most important to your potential client. That would often allow you to anticipate questions the client would ask, which meant you could have a well-prepared answer and solution to their problems or concerns.

Second, you set the expectations for the presentation itself. You start off the presentation by telling them exactly what you're going to do, how you're going to do it, and how long each segment of the presentation will take. An example might go something like this, "For the first thirty minutes of our presentation, we will discuss the health benefit package we can offer to your employees. That will be followed by five minutes of Q & A. Next, we will spend fifteen minutes discussing basic life insurance packages, followed by five minutes of Q & A, and then a short break."

If you don't set expectations, you run the risk of your audience getting bored, impatient, or disengaged. At some point in your presentation, if they don't feel the topic is particularly interesting, or if they already know everything you're saying, it's important for them to realize there is only three minutes left in that particular segment. Otherwise, they may become anxious—especially if they don't know how long you're going to stay on a particular topic.

That brings me to my next point. You have to read your audience. With their looks, their body language, and maybe their questions, the audience will tell you how much interest, or lack of interest, they have in a particular topic. A topic may have seemed very important in the RFP, but if you've addressed all of their concerns in the first ten minutes—and they're satisfied and happy with what you've given them—maybe it's time to move on even though you originally planned for ten more minutes of slides. It's important not just to read your audience, but to respond and be flexible. Their questions, facial expressions, and body language could alert you to the fact that they're wanting to spend more or less time on a different topic.

This presentation was different. I wasn't reading normal business interactions. As we got going, the president of the company was asking a lot of questions, but he directed all of his questions to Bill. He still was not acknowledging me.

I was the senior member of the team in this situation so most of the time, Bill could not answer, or he was wise enough to know he shouldn't answer. That being the case, Bill would politely refer the vast majority of the questions to me.

Patiently and politely, I would answer each question. Never once did I display a hostile attitude of any kind. I never pulled rank or let my ego get in the way by saying things like, "Hey, you really need to talk to me about that." I did not display frustration or impatience at the man's lack of respect toward me.

My attitude toward this man was basically, "I'm not going to allow you to hate me."

I'd taken that attitude many times in my life, and I would continue to do that every time the opportunity presented itself. You might say it has been one of my core principles in regard to the issue of racial equality. No matter how determined a person is to hate me, I can be even more determined to set them free of that hate.

This dance continued for almost the full hour-long presentation. Finally, something seemed to break. After about 45 minutes of me skillfully, patiently, and tactfully answering this man's questions, he finally looked my way and directed a question toward me. Then another. I answered both questions with precision and prowess.

At that point, the benefit director spoke up and said, "I don't care how good you guys are, if you're one penny more expensive than the other companies, we won't be buying anything from you."

He made it crystal clear that price was going to be *the* determining factor in their decision. The broker had already told us that price was a high priority item, and I knew that we were priced higher than the competition.

By that point in my career, I had already learned an extremely important principle—that price is only an issue in the absence of value. When you convey enough value to a person, price moves down the priority list. Sometimes it moves way down. It can even become a non-issue if you convey enough value.

God has blessed me with opportunities to teach this principle to many others during my career. The example I often use is Saks Fifth Avenue. Saks Fifth Avenue can sell a basic white dress shirt for $200. I've bought tons of them over the years. JC Penney sells a similar white dress shirt for $29. Saks sells plenty of white dress shirts for $200, and they make plenty of profit doing it.

Why would anyone pay $200 for a shirt that's really similar to one you can get for $29? Because they perceive value in the $200 shirt, and they're willing to pay for that value. Young salespeople who don't understand this principle will tend to panic a little when a potential customer makes such a strong statement about price. Their immediate reaction is to start asking, "How can we cut the price?"

My response to the benefit director was, "I'd like to talk about price at the end of the presentation."

He said something like, "Well, you're going to have to cut your price, because it's too high."

Politely and patiently, I responded again, "Well, let's wait until the end to address the issue of price."

We continued our presentation. From that point on, the president of the company looked me in the eye and directed every single question to me. Once the presentation was concluded and I'd answered every question to his satisfaction, this company president stood up, looked at me and said, "Good job."

He looked over at the broker and announced, "We're going to buy from them."

The issue of price never came up again.

The company president—an active imperial wizard for the KKK—got out of his seat, walked over to me, shook my hand and stated again, "We're buying from you."

I can't say for sure if this man now liked me, but I can tell you that he respected me from that point forward.

A BANK EXECUTIVE HAS HIS PREJUDICES
CHALLENGED

In addition to being a victory for the advancement of racial equality, my sales meeting with the KKK wizard was also a personal milestone. Years before, when I was brand new in my career, I'd had that sales meeting with another man who was known to be blatantly racist.

The end result was failure, and Marshall had tried to

assuage my pain by chalking my failure up to the man's racism. That excuse would have allowed me to be more at peace with myself in that moment. I might have felt a little better when I went home that night.

But if I had accepted and internalized that excuse for my failure, I never would have dealt with my own responsibility. The truth is that I *could* sell insurance contracts to racist people—if I was prepared well enough. Making excuses for my failure would have been to my own detriment. It would not have hurt the racist who didn't buy from me. It would have only hurt me.

Being able to sell the KKK imperial wizard for Middle Tennessee was proof positive that even the worst cases of racism could not limit my success. If I did my job well enough, nothing could stop me. The lesson there is, "Be so good that they can't deny you."

If you're a minority, you'll personally benefit by adopting this attitude, and you'll also help advance racial equality in the process. In fact, by being your best, you'll advance racial equality just about on a daily basis, even when you're unaware that it's happening. You'll open doors for yourself and for others. If you continue to work hard and grow your skills, there is no limit to what you can accomplish.

This next story provides a rare glimpse into what happens when a minority person exceeds everyone's expectations—breaking down racial prejudices that people may not even realize they're carrying.

Around 1988, I was down in Florida doing a sales pitch for a large commercial bank—the largest bank in Florida at that time. We were looking to write health insurance policies that would cover all of the bank's employees, so it was a very large contract. In fact, if I were to get the contract, it would be the largest sale of my career up to that point.

The award of the contract had been narrowed down to us and two other companies. The company I represented—Provident—was well established, but the other two companies were powerhouses in the insurance industry, both with household names.

My team and I came in and did the presentation. As was our usual setup, I led the presentation because I was the sales executive in charge of the team. We had gone through tons of mock presentations and Q & A. We were extremely well-prepared, and we nailed it.

We were awarded the business and went out to dinner that night with the executives from the bank. One of the vice presidents called me aside at that dinner and said, "We were very happy to award you the business. But I wanted you to know that so much of it was due to your presentation."

I smiled and nodded, happy to receive both the business and the positive feedback.

He continued, "I don't want to offend you, but I gotta ask you—Where did you come from?"

Not knowing exactly how to respond, I just responded with humor, "What do you mean? I came from my mama and daddy, just like you did." I smiled, trying to hide any discomfort I felt at this strange question.

"No, seriously. Where did you come from? I've been in this business a long time, and I've never seen a Black man walk into a room and command a room like that. I've never seen a Black man lead like that or speak with such power and conviction.

"You articulated everything perfectly, and everyone listened intently. You had such good wisdom, and you shared such vision. And in the last five minutes, you perfectly recapped an intense two-hour meeting. You did all of this without using a single note of any kind. When it was over, my team and I were all asking, 'Where did this guy come from?'"

This man's perception of Black people was being shattered.

You could hear it in his voice—he was genuinely shocked at what he had seen that day. He wanted some kind of explanation for it. He wanted to understand how this was possible. Everything he had believed his entire life—and probably everything he had been taught—about Black people was being challenged. The funny thing is, he loved it!

He wasn't upset that his prejudices were being shattered. He seemed to relish the idea. This man even discussed the whole issue with the other people on his team, like he'd just found some wonderful new insight that they should all grab hold of. He was effectively telling everyone around him, "Hey, Black people can be incredibly smart and capable too! Who knew!?!"

He was liberated from some wrong prejudices that day. We'll probably never know this side of Heaven how many times I'd done that same thing for others, and I just didn't get the follow up comments from them.

In this day and time, a Black person would rightly be offended at such a line of questioning. Everyone is supposed to have moved beyond such archaic reasoning. But this kind of thinking was almost a given early in my career. There was no reason for me to be upset with him about being honest.

I was just glad to be the one shattering his false beliefs.

13

AMERICA'S COUNTRY CLUBS: BLACK GOLFERS NEED NOT APPLY

The decision to advance myself in predominantly white society, business, and culture was intentional. And it was missional. As I've stated several times, I was often acting in self-interest. Being my best and achieving all I could achieve. But I also knew that in the process, I was breaking barriers and opening doors that would help advance racial equality.

As fate—or maybe providence—would have it, we often chose to live in communities that were predominantly white. We often chose to attend predominantly white churches. It just so happened that we sent our children to predominantly white schools, sometimes public, sometimes private. We didn't set out to be in predominantly white places or to avoid other Black people. That was not our intent, but people in the Black community tended to question whether we were intentionally running away from Black communities, and we had to live with that criticism.

Besides having to deal with the challenge of criticism, being the only Black person, or one of very few Black people, everywhere we went wasn't always the most comfortable thing in the world for us. But it was the most beneficial, both for us personally and for racial equality. The truth is, integration was needed just about everywhere we looked, and we always felt a call to rise to that challenge.

We certainly had an awareness that we could help break barriers and stereotypes in many aspects of society. At the same time, we wanted to put our daughters, Deidre and Rashele, in the best schools, and that often meant putting them in predominantly white schools.

We never sat down and asked ourselves, "Where is the whitest school we can find?" We asked, "What is the best school in this community?" Things are starting to change now, but back then the answer almost always involved a predominantly white school. So when faced with that situation, it really was like killing two birds with one stone. We could advance the cause of Black equality while also having the best for our daughters.

Of course, we wanted the best for all aspects of our life, not just our kids' schools. So over and over, we experienced this principle that we could advance racial equality often by simply doing what was best for ourselves, even if we had to deal with some discomfort and challenges along the way.

One really good example of the progress that was ushered in through our personal choices came in 1984. Back when I had first gotten into the business world, I was told, "You have to learn to play golf." But I had zero interest in golf.

Quite frankly, I thought of golf as a white man's game. It also did not look very fun to me, so I just wasn't interested at all. But all of my superiors hounded me about it. They even claimed that learning golf would be the *number one* tool I could use to be successful.

Enough said.

I began learning the game, often entertaining clients on the golf course, and I found that my superiors were absolutely correct. In business school, they prepare you very well to handle business interviews, dinners, and those types of conversations. One thing I learned is that people are different in those settings.

With the same person, I can go to business meeting after business meeting. We can go to multiple dinners together, and that person will never reveal to me anything that they did not purposefully plan to reveal to me. In those settings, a professional businessperson has a certain guard up, and will never tell me anything they didn't already want me to know.

At a dinner, a person may talk a little about their family. They may tell you about their dog. But they'll never reveal anything truly important about themselves.

But the same person, I can take out for one round of golf and learn more about them as a person than I could in a hundred boardroom meetings. They would share things on the golf course that they never would have told me in the boardroom or at the dinner table.

Two things happen in golf that make this possible. People hit the ball really well, and they get very excited. Their adrenaline and endorphins are released, and they're charged up. When that's the case, they tend to open up more.

Conversely, they may not be very good. In that case, they end up angry and frustrated. All of a sudden, they don't have to pretend to be invincible anymore. They become a person who acknowledges that they have weaknesses. They might even ask for help.

Either way, I'm now dealing with a human being who is willing to be vulnerable, and vulnerability makes all the difference in the world when it comes to truly connecting with a person. So the game of golf has been incredibly helpful to me in my business career over the years.

When I first moved to the Atlanta area in 1983, I needed a place to play golf. We looked around and found that none of the clubs we looked into would allow Black members. After further investigation, we finally found that there were two clubs in the Atlanta area that would allow Black members.

One of them was really close to our house in Cobb County. Indian Hills Country Club was less than two miles from where we lived, so in 1984, I joined Indian Hills Country Club. They had around five Black members at the time.

It was not the top golf course in town, but it was really nice and I could take my customers to play golf there. Along with my customers and friends, I enjoyed Indian Hills for many years.

Fast forward to 1990, and Shoal Creek Club in Birmingham, Alabama, was set to host the PGA Championship. But there was a huge problem and it started getting some attention in the media: Shoal Creek had no Black members. A reporter for the Birmingham Post-Herald interviewed the club founder, Hall Thompson, and got this quote, "We have the right to associate or not to associate with whomever we choose. The country club is our home and we pick and choose who we want. I think we've said that we don't discriminate in every other area except the Blacks."[1]

While many clubs quietly refused African American members back then, this man had made the mistake of giving a quote people could use to push back. There was an uprising in the world of golf.

People began to boycott the PGA. Sponsors pulled out. And the world of golf was forced to deal with this issue.

Eventually, the PGA decided that they would not be taking their tournament or events to any club that did not have Black members. All at once, the best clubs in Atlanta were actively looking for Black members. At the same time, Provident had recently promoted me to a new position and began urging me to find a more prestigious club to host clients. It would have been best for my business to be at the best club, so I was happy to look at some of the other clubs.

All of these wonderful golf clubs that previously wouldn't let me in the door were now courting me to become a member at their club. Every major golf course in Atlanta contacted me about joining their club, but Atlanta Country Club was and is the best, in my opinion. They also happened to be very close to my house. Some of the other clubs would have meant fighting 45 minutes or so of traffic.

Atlanta Country Club had some of the most prestigious members too. All things considered, it was going to be the best choice for me, my business, and my family.

After making my choice, I was all set to become the first ever Black member of Atlanta Country Club. The club had some PR reasons for doing this, of course. Unexpectedly, I got a phone call from one of their members a day or so before I was set to officially join.

He explained that their board had talked it over some more and decided to bring in a different Black person first. They still wanted me to join, but for the purposes of their press coverage, they thought that this other Black man, Eula

Adams, who had been a successful accountant, would be a better choice.

Their reason was that I had been a college athlete, and they didn't want it to seem like they'd just gone out and found a Black athlete to join. They basically were concerned that they'd be unfairly criticized in the press for my status as a former football player.

They didn't mandate the change, but basically asked, "If you're okay with it, we'd like for you to wait a week or so in order to let us bring in this other person first."

I said, "Sure, that's no problem."

I was not trying to make any headlines. I didn't care about press releases or publicity. The whole decision for me had been about what was best for me, my family, and my business.

The other new member, Eula, stayed at the club for a couple of years before moving to Denver. For seven or eight years after Eula left, I was the only Black member at the Atlanta Country Club.

The Atlanta Journal-Constitution actually wrote an article in 1997 which was all about my experience as the lone Black member. It was in a special section they did about the advancement of Black people in the world of golf. The title of the article was "Comfort is key, exec says."[2] The "comfort" refers to becoming comfortable as the only Black person in an environment with hundreds of other people. Basically, you look different than everyone else, and the experience is not always easy or comfortable. But if you are comfortable with yourself, and confident in yourself, you will be able to better navigate those kinds of situations.

During those years, I hope and believe I made an impact in regard to people's prejudices. I remember when I first went to pay my membership dues, the initial fee at that time was $37,500. The people at the club didn't know me, and didn't know all that much about me. They knew that I was an insurance executive but that was about it. They didn't know a lot about my finances.

So when it came time for me to do the paperwork, they seemed a little nervous. "We have this really large initial fee to join the club, and after that we have annual dues. We really want you here, so if you can just pay the annual dues, we will allow you to pay the initiation fee in installments . . ."

Atlanta Country Club has members who are multimillionaires and even billionaires. So to them, maybe I just looked like a small potatoes Black guy who didn't have $37,500.

"Guys, if I couldn't pay the bill, I wouldn't be here."

There's no way I was about to let anyone view me as a charity case, or a partial member. If I was going to be a member there, I was going to be a full-fledged member with full rights and privileges. No one was going to be treating me like a second-class citizen. I was going to have the same right to be there as everyone else.

So I continued, "Whatever the number is, just tell me and I'll have a check to you this afternoon. I want to pay every fee that is due. I want to pay them in full. And I want to pay them now. Because the first time a person comes up and says something inappropriate to me, I'll be letting them know I have just as much right to be here as they do. So you tell me the number and I'll pay it immediately. I don't care what it is."

They told me the number and I took over a check. I guess it just takes some people a while to get over things, because the man who took my check actually said, "Okay, do I need to wait a day or two before cashing this?"

"Mister, you can take that check and cash it in the next two minutes."

When you're the first Black guy—or one of the first—to do a particular thing, you're going to run into awkward situations like that. Initially, there were some members that refused to speak to me or acknowledge me. They wanted me to know that they would prefer me not being there, so they made it obvious. You get that just about anywhere you go when you're one of the first Black people to have gone to a certain place or done a particular thing.

But overall, most of the members were extremely nice, kind, and friendly with me. You get a lot of that too.

What's so neat is that in these situations, you see the racist person actually get relegated into silence over time. They used to have the accepted view, but now they don't. They are trying to come to grips with that, so at first, they're just starting to realize that their view is no longer predominant.

However, they still feel comfortable in expressing their prejudices through passive aggressive means. After enough time, the overall group has made their decision. They've taken their stand, and racism is no longer to be tolerated in any form. This is the way it is, and everyone knows it. On top of that, you've won them over on a personal level.

Anyone still holding onto racism at that point now has to hide it. They are actually made to feel ashamed of their racist attitudes, and that's of course exactly how it should be.

I'll never forget the first day I played golf at Atlanta Country Club. It was about 10:30 on a Saturday morning, which is a very busy time for the club. I was playing with a group called "The Scratch Group Golfers." There were people all around, some getting warmed up. Others were on the putting green waiting to tee off. Some people were sitting on a large balcony deck that overlooks the first tee and the green.

I'm not sure if Eula had already been to the club for a round of golf yet or not. All I know is that there was a lot of interest in my round of golf that day. By the time I was ready to tee off, that back balcony was completely full of people. Everyone down on the ground seemed to stop what they were doing to observe this spectacle of the Black guy teeing off for the first time at Atlanta Country Club.

The caddies and caddy masters—two of which were Black—all came out to watch. I don't necessarily think anyone was trying to intimidate me, but they certainly knew that the pressure would be on with all of those eyes watching. So while they may not have been purposefully trying to intimidate me, they weren't cutting me any slack either.

Fortunately for me, it was one of those days when my game was on point. Stepping up to the first tee, I focused, breathed in, drew back, and *whack*! The ball sailed about 280 yards straight  as an arrow down the fairway. It was an absolutely perfect shot.

A member of the club named Lynn Hughes was standing nearby. Lynn had been the starting quarterback for the University of Georgia during his sophomore year, before splitting his time on offense and defense during his junior and senior years, eventually becoming an All-American safety in 1966. He later ended up playing in the Canadian Football League. Lynn was a reasonably well-known figure around Atlanta at that time.

Right after my shot, Lynn came up to me and bear hugged me right there on the tee. He said, "That was powerful! You just made a statement to this membership that you can play, and you're not going to back off no matter what!"

I have now been a member of Atlanta Country Club for 30 years. I've served on the board of directors, the greens committee, the golf committee, and the long-range planning committee. I've been one of the lead members of the club, and was instrumental in all of our major hiring, our strategic direction, and other aspects of the club for many years.

During that time, my membership in the club has benefited me tremendously—both at a personal and professional level. I like to think I've benefited the club as well. The friends that I've made, and the relationships I've built are invaluable.

Enduring a few awkward moments, condescending attitudes, or disdainful looks was well worth the benefits to me personally, to my business and family, and to my race.

THE WORLD OF GOLF: INTEGRATION NEEDED EVERYWHERE

Golf is a very unique game that teaches a lot of valuable life skills to young people, and reinforces those same skills in adults. For example, in football, if the receiver knows he didn't catch the ball, but he almost caught it, what does he do? He gets up and starts trying to convince everyone that he caught it.

If the defensive back grabbed the receiver way before the ball got there, and he knows he did, what does he do? He gets up trying to convince everyone, especially the refs, that he didn't do anything wrong.

It's the same in boxing. In baseball. In just about every other sport.

But golf is the opposite. You hit your ball in the woods, your competitors aren't supposed to follow you in there. Why? Because everyone in golf is expected to be honest, and the vast majority of people are. It is said to be a gentlemen's game.

You go into the woods and you play it where it lies, just like the rules say to. That's the game of golf. It's the only serious game I know of where players keep their own score.

It's also a game where you can really get to know people and form healthy friendships. There are many benefits to the game of golf, and I would encourage young people to seriously give the game a try.

I've been very blessed in my life to be able to play at most of the world's top clubs. People who are really serious about golf normally have a bucket list of playing at some of the world's best clubs. Maybe playing at the Augusta National Golf Club, or attending the The Masters Tournament in Augusta, Georgia.

God has blessed me to attend the tournament 30 out of the last 41 years. I've played at pretty much every elite club in the country. Augusta National. Pine Valley. Cypress Point. Pebble Beach. San Francisco Golf Club. Chicago Golf Club. Pretty much all of the top 10 courses. All of the Long Island clubs. For the last 15 years, I've been an official rater for Golf Digest, so I'm actually involved in rating the courses to determine which ones are the nation's best.

Beyond the continental US, I've played at places all around the world, including quite a few of the world's top courses. Royal County Down Golf Club in Ireland is widely considered to be the world's #1 golf course. I've been privileged to play there. Muirfield is one of the most renowned clubs on the planet, and I've played there. The oldest club in the world (and one of the best) is St. Andrews Old in Scotland, and I've been privileged to play there.

I've played in Cancun. Hawaii. Puerto Rico. All over the world—You get the point.

But the real point is not for me to brag about all the top courses where I've played. When I play those places, I'm treated extremely well. There is no perceivable difference between how I'm treated and how white people are treated. The best clubs welcome me, take good care of me, and accommodate me any way they can. They roll out the red carpet for me just like they do any other guest. They don't seem to pay any attention to my race.

Unfortunately, that's not true for every golf course.

For many years, as I've played all around the country, I've noticed that the municipal, lower-level, and middle-income type of country clubs have not treated me so well. Some of them can treat a Black person very nasty. I've had quite a few encounters with such attitudes and behaviors over the years.

To make the point, I'll just give one example.

On a Saturday morning in 2002, my wife and I were in another state visiting some of her friends. Thinking it would be nice to let the girls have some fun together, I decided to go to the local community course and see if I could get into a golf game.

When I got there, I realized I was the only Black person at the club that day. This wasn't really out of the ordinary.

While golf has gotten more integrated over the years, it's still not uncommon for me to be the only Black person on that day when I'm playing at various courses. Anyway, I got there and told them I wanted to get into a game that morning.

The people looked at me like I was from Mars. It was obvious they felt very uncomfortable about me being there. I said to the course pro, "Look, I don't want to disrupt anything. I just thought if you have a slot for a single, I'd like to play."

He says, "Yeah, we have a slot, but you have to play in our gambling game. We have it every Saturday morning, and it's the only thing we have in the morning."

There were about 30 guys gathered for the game. It was nothing major. Everyone puts in $20 or so, and the top 3 golfers split the pot. I said, "Okay, I really don't want to do that. But if that's the only way I can play, I'll play."

As I was getting put into the game, they asked me, "Ralph, what's your handicap?"

"Guys, I'm a pretty good golfer. Right now, my handicap is 4 . . . "

I wanted to be completely upfront with them. My game was really on point at that time, so I continued, " . . . but I'm actually playing pretty well right now. Maybe even a little better than 4."

They said, "No problem, we'll put you down at 4."

I agreed, and even showed them my United States Golf Association numbers that shows all my scores and how my handicap was derived. So everyone was on the same page when we went out.

What can I say—I had pretty good day. On a golf course I've never seen before, I went out and I believe I shot a 75. For those of you who don't know golf, that's pretty good. A lower score is better, and 70-72 is the best you can get, depending on the specific course.

I finished second overall out of the 30 guys who played the gambling round that morning. You would have thought I murdered somebody the way they were treating me.

They basically acted like I was a criminal who came in there and hustled them for money.

Nevermind that I didn't even want to gamble. All I wanted to do was play golf. All that seemed to have been forgotten. I said, "Guys, I don't want your money. You can keep it."

That only made them more angry. Now I was insulting them by turning them into a charity case. There seemed to be no way for me to win.

Just when I didn't think it could get any worse, this one guy announces to everyone that his wedding ring is missing. Then he walked right over to me and said, "You stole my wedding ring."

"Mister, I didn't steal anything."

"Well, I need to search your bag."

This was during the time when I was the Senior Vice President of Sales and Marketing for a Fortune 500 company. But I didn't play that card. I never play the status card with people like this man. Doing that might help me win the battle that day, but I don't think that's the right way to win the war. So I respond by doing what I always do.

I respond respectfully.

I treat him how I wanted to be treated. With dignity and respect.

"Look, that's no problem. I can see that you're having an issue here, so you can search my bag."

He actually searched my bag.

But he still wasn't satisfied. The guy who lost his wedding ring was convinced that the Black man must have stolen it. He said, "I need to search everything you've got."

"Okay. Go ahead."

I had not even met this guy or been close to him on the course. It was shocking, but I recognized that the man had a problem. He had some prejudices, and he needed me to help him see the light.

I let him search everything, and I was as nice as I knew how to be to him. I knew that cursing him or fighting him would not help me. And it wouldn't help him either. I wanted to do whatever I could to let him know that I didn't have his ring. But I also wanted to make sure I didn't lower myself to his level of anger or hatred.

I can honestly say that I hope he found his ring. Ultimately, I don't know if I changed anything in this man's mind and heart on that particular day. But maybe later on, something got through to him about the way he treated me versus the way I responded.

Some people may disagree with my approach, and that's fine. I understand that, and maybe it's not for everyone. But I have found that over time, it's a very effective way to strip racist attitudes from people's minds and hearts.

This is especially true when it comes to golf. The golf community is very passionate. When you can show them that you love and respect the game they love and respect, you can often win them over. You find common ground—a shared passion—and you end up winning their respect.

I would say that *most of the time*, someone who truly loves golf will get beyond their attitude of prejudice once you show them that you are serious about golf. Sometimes, you almost get to see their prejudice disappear right in front of your face. It usually takes a while to get there, but when it does get there, it's worth all the difficulty and pain.

Unfortunately, the situation often starts out like the one I described earlier. The lower tier courses in America still seem to have issues with prejudice.

My friend John Covington commented that when he calls a CEO, he pretty much always gets a call back. But sometimes if he calls a middle management professional, he won't get a call back. His theory is that the CEO respects and values other people, whereas the middle management professional really doesn't—and that's why they're both in the position they're in.

Top courses are top courses for a lot of reasons, so it might not be a perfect metaphor. But to be sure, organizations that develop a culture of inclusivity, respect, human dignity, and equality are going to rise to the top, while the rest will languish in mediocrity.

So I would encourage anyone reading that if you want your organization to be the cream that rises to the top, get out and take the lead on this issue.

I would simultaneously encourage minorities everywhere to consider going even to those places where it's not comfortable. Where you're not always warmly welcomed. Because through your outstanding character, your attitude of excellence, and your high moral standards, you can bring positive change to the world you live in.

14

DON'T ALLOW ANYONE TO HATE YOU

As I recently recounted some of these events in my life, a friend asked me if it bothered me that I was often the only Black guy around. The reality of that situation can't be exaggerated. While playing football at Robert E. Lee and later at Alabama, I had gotten used to being one of the few Black people around.

But when I entered my career, I was the *only one* around for many years. I would go to a business convention or training and be sitting in a room of 300 people. Looking around, I'd most often be the only Black person in the room.

The short answer to my friend's question is "Yes." In that situation, you are very much aware that you stand out. That you're different.

And back then, especially in the 70s and 80s, people were still much more bold about their racism. They would often let you know that they really didn't want you around. More times than I care to recount, I had to endure people loudly saying the n-word at cocktail parties, making racist jokes, or saying otherwise inappropriate and hurtful things.

Often, the person was doing it purposefully. They wanted me to hear, and they wanted me to feel uncomfortable—unwelcome, in fact.

At that point, you always have a decision to make. Do I go address this somehow? Do I ignore it? These can be hard decisions. The choice you make can affect you, your family, and your career in significant ways.

But there are times you have to confront people about wrong behavior, and I did that on many occasions. The key is to know when to confront and when to let it go. You can't walk away at all times, and you can't confront at all times. One thing you *can* always do is be in control of your own response.

Like everyone else on the planet, I have a temper. And if I'm not careful, I could easily lose my temper and react to these kinds of situations in anger. But self-control is always the better choice.

One thing I learned early in life is that I cannot beat prejudice out of a human being. So if someone calls me the n-word and then I go and exchange blows with them—win or lose—I'm not going to change their racist attitudes. They will walk away with the same hatred and biases they had before our encounter.

In fact, that person will probably feel that their prejudices have been reinforced. When you respond to racist attitudes with physical violence, you are allowing that person to continue hating you.

The same is true for a yelling match. The same is true for a verbal beating or cursing. If I let a racist person have it in that way, it's not going to eliminate any of the wrong attitudes from that person's heart and mind.

But many times in my life, I have seen racist attitudes

driven from people's minds and hearts, and the method is always the same.

Prove them wrong.

That's how you refuse to let someone else hate you. You conduct yourself in such a way that hate is no longer an option. Going into many environments in my life where Black people traditionally had not been invited, my approach has always been to conduct myself in a way that is completely contrary to bigoted views.

- *Black people are violent*—wrong.
- *Black people can't have a civilized conversation when topics become charged or relations become strained* —wrong.
- *Black people can't conduct themselves in a professional manner at all times*—wrong.
- *Black people aren't intelligent enough to do this job* —wrong.
- *Black people are morally deficient*—wrong.
- *Black people are inferior*—wrong.

For so many white people I've encountered in life, their perception was that Black people just couldn't do things right. So I always wanted to be an example of doing it right. I want to live my life in such a way that every time you see me, hear me, or hear of me, it's because I'm doing something right. Now I'm human, and I fall short plenty of the time. But my attitude is to always do my best.

Whatever the particulars of each bigoted mindset you run into, you have an opportunity to obliterate that mindset through your conduct and your character. To do so is the loving choice. The bigot will be better off when they are set free. You will be better off through personal advancement and character building. And the world will be better off because a little bit of hatred died that day.

So anytime you're confronted with bigotry, you basically have the opportunity to overcome hatred with love.

Developing that mindset will set you up with a major key for victory in these situations. Instead of telling people how wrong they are, show them how wrong they are. You will benefit yourself in the process. You and others like you will advance in the world, while the people who harbor racist attitudes will continue to diminish in power and influence.

All of this really goes back to a very simple, key principle that my mother always instilled in us: "**Don't lower yourself down to their level.**"

At the same time, I want to be very clear about something. I am not advocating that you ever make yourself a doormat. What I'm trying to impart is that there are ways to challenge bigotry that are more effective. So *how* we challenge bigotry is important, but what we should never do is simply accept it.

Another major key to overcoming the challenges of bigotry is to become comfortable in your own skin. The more you make right choices, and the more you rise above the hatred, the more confident you will feel about who you are as a person. You'll *know* that any bigoted opinions of you are wrong.

You can also know that God says you are fearfully and wonderfully made. You are His masterpiece, and no one can take that away from you. Once you really get those truths down in your spirit, it becomes easier to withstand the attacks of prejudice and bigotry.

MAKING AN IMPACT CAN BE SIMPLE

You don't have to seek out bigoted, nasty people, but you don't have to completely avoid them either. Say for example that you're at a business conference. You hear someone openly and intentionally make a racist comment. A couple of days later, you find out you're seated at a luncheon with that same person.

Are you going to get up and leave the table?

I'm not going to leave that table. In fact, I'm going to be at that table fully engaged in the conversation. And hopefully, me and that guy with the bigotry problem will end up talking. Ideally, we'll find some common ground and it will give me a chance to make a positive impact on someone who needs my help.

By the end of the lunch, if he's looking at me just a little bit different than he was looking at me before the lunch, then I've had a positive impact on the world—simply by having lunch.

A MAJOR WAY TO GET IT RIGHT

In the first chapter, I mentioned that my dad often told us, "Do right and right will follow you." What he meant by that is, "If you do right, you will find that the right things end up happening in your life." It's a great principle, and one that I've often repeated to my own daughters.

Of course, we don't just repeat the saying. We seek to live by those words. Over the years when I would remind them of this truth, my daughters would often respond, "Yes, right follows. But not as close as we would like it to." My daughters are correct in their assessment. We don't always get to see the fruit of our labors immediately. But God has a way of making sure that we reap what we sow.

That saying, "reap what you sow" is a metaphor. It's referring to the fact that a farmer will harvest (reap) the crops of whatever seed he plants (sows) in the ground. It's the same in life. If you consistently try to do what is right and good, the harvest of your life will usually be right and good.

One of the major ways our family focuses on getting it right is to be generous with our time, talents, and resources. Giving back is at the core of our value system.

As a young man, I began serving as a volunteer with several charities. The more I grew and prospered in business, the more opportunities I found to give back. I have served on the board of directors for organizations like the YMCA, the Cystic Fibrosis Foundation, the BellSouth Golf Classic (a charity golf tournament), and Special Olympics Georgia. I've served on the committees of several other organizations, and for three years, I even led a goal setting class at MUST Ministries, a homeless shelter in Marietta, Georgia.

My wife Debra lives out these values as well. She serves on the board of Your Working Copy, Inc., an audio Bible ministry. She serves at another ministry that supports women and children who find themselves in temporary housing situations. In the past, she also served at MUST Ministries.

Our daughters carry the legacy of giving and serving. Deidre, our oldest, started in high school participating in AIDS walks to raise money for AIDS research and patient care. She also serves on the board of Your Working Copy, Inc. As an attorney, she has donated time to the Innocence Project, which works to help people who were wrongfully convicted.

Rashele, our younger daughter, has always had a heart for animals. She started volunteering in middle school with the Humane Society. Over the last 20 years she has fostered hundreds of dogs, a passion she now shares with her two daughters.

Of all the charities our family has been involved with, Special Olympics Georgia has probably been the most near and dear to our hearts. Every year, Special Olympics Georgia hosts their big, Olympic-style event with more than 1000 kids from all over the state of Georgia. Every year, I am moved to tears at the torch lighting ceremony. The spirit, dedication, and skill of these young athletes is very heart warming.

To any young person looking to succeed in life, I would encourage you to do something that might be counterintuitive to you right now. You have to find something you are passionate about and learn to give back. This is crucial to any person's well-being, and it will help you become a more successful person. I'm not talking about the business and social connections you will make by participating with charities and ministries. Those things are there, but they are not the driving motivation.

What I'm talking about is the change inside of a human being who gives of their time, talent, and treasure to serve others. When you serve, give, and love others, you are sowing the right seeds and you will reap a good harvest.

Right will follow you!

LISTENING TO GOD'S VOICE

A s you move through your journey of life, sometimes you will hear God's voice prompting you to move in a different direction. All of a sudden, a completely unexpected move comes to mind and you won't be able to shake it. You'll know He's pointing you to do something that's different from what you had planned.

That's how it happened for me, and in a very dramatic way.

The year was 2003 and I was in the middle of living out my professional dreams. As Senior Vice President in charge of sales and marketing for a major health insurance company —Cigna Healthcare of Georgia and Alabama—I had seemingly reached the pinnacle of my career. A huge corner office. Status. A great personal assistant. Corporate perks. Prestige. Money. Wonderful business relationships.

I'd been in the business for 27 years, and had occupied my current position successfully for the previous 6 years.

One day, I was sitting in my office and out of nowhere, I heard the words, "It's time to leave this job." I looked all around the office. I even looked behind me. No one was in the room with me.

So I walked out of my office to my assistant's desk.

"Kathy, did you say something to me?"

"No, I didn't say anything."

"Okay . . . I thought I heard something."

Thinking I must have just overheard someone else's conversation, I walked back into my office and sat down.

About 5 to 10 minutes later, I heard it again. Only this time, I couldn't mistake it as being another person's conversation.

"Ralph, it's time to leave this job."

I sat there quietly. Still. Not knowing what to make of this, I did the only thing that made sense to me. I pointed my attention toward the person in closest proximity to me.

"Kathy?" I called out. "What did you just say to me?"

This time she responded with a mix of confusion and frustration. "What are you bothering me for? I didn't say anything. Nobody's been by here. Nobody's saying anything to you. What are you talking about?!?"

At that point I wasn't sure what to think or what to say. I heard that statement. I heard those words as sure as my name is Ralph Stokes. Looking back on it, I can't say that I heard a male voice or a female voice. I just heard a voice. In that moment, all I knew to do was shake it off and try to settle back into work.

After a few minutes, I heard it one more time.

"Ralph, it is time to leave this job." This time it was spoken with conviction and emphasis—the same way your father would say something to you when he had to tell you for the third time.

Just like the prophet Samuel when he was a young boy

hearing a voice call out to him in the night, I guess I was a little slow in catching on to what was happening. Because I did the same thing he did. I kept getting up and going to the person in the next room, asking them what they wanted.

"Kathy, I know you said something . . . "

"Ralph, you must be having some kind of breakdown because I have not said anything to you. Nobody has stopped by here. Nobody has walked by this office. So you figure out what's going on with *you*."

Well, she was partly right. There was something going on with me. But it wasn't just me, and I finally understood that. The next words out of my mouth were, "God . . . I . . . I have clearly heard You say that it's time for me to leave this job."

I can't say that it was an audible physical voice that I heard. But I did hear it. I don't know how else to explain it. In the Bible, there are examples of people hearing things with their spirit, just like Samuel did. There are also examples of people seeing things with their spirit, just like Elijah and Elisha did.

If you ask me what happened, my best guess is that God spoke those words to me, and my spirit man was enabled to hear them loudly and clearly.

But that day, I didn't have any concept of hearing something with my spirit. I just struggled to make sense of it, so I began confessing that struggle to God and asking for His help.

"God, I don't know. I mean, it sure sounded like You were telling me it is time to leave this job. But if that was You, will You please give me clear verification that it was You?"

DIVINE CONFIRMATION

That night, when I went home, my oldest brother, Frank Stokes Jr., called me out of the blue. As I mentioned previously, Frank was absolutely brilliant, with his IQ of 161. But he didn't do well at personal interaction with everyday people. He would explain something to the people who worked with him or under him, and they wouldn't get it. And he didn't get why they didn't get it.

Things that were almost effortless for him would be difficult for others, and he just couldn't understand that. He also struggled to explain things in a way that the average person would understand. All of that led to serious frustration for him.

After a while, he and his wife made a decision that he would stay home and raise the kids. She would work as a nurse.

There's nothing wrong with their decision. Their decision worked out extremely well for their family, as Frank's children are all brilliant and successful themselves. It was the best decision for their family, and I always respected it. And I always respected Frank. Besides being a genius, he was just an all-around great person. But his family and vocational choice left him feeling very insecure.

Any time I ever asked for his advice, he would say, "You and Theron know better than I do. You're the ones who are successful."

I always hated that he saw himself that way. I did not see him that way, and always wanted his advice. He was the smartest one in our family, after all. But I could never get him to give me any advice. He just didn't see his own value.

Well, this day was the lone exception. While I normally

could not get Frank Jr. to give me advice even by begging for it, this day he called and gave me some completely unsolicited advice.

"Hey, Ralph! How's it going?"

"Hey, Frank! It's going well. How are you?"

"Doing well. Ralph, I just wanted to call you and let you know, it's time for you to leave that job. It's time for you to leave Cigna."

I was caught completely off guard. This is the man who refused to give me advice even if I was twisting his arm.

I mustered a response. "Okay . . . well . . . why would you say that, Frank? Why would you call me out of the blue and tell me to leave my job?"

At this point, he sounded very surprised himself. "Truly, Ralph, I don't know. I have no idea why I called you to tell you that . . . it was just something that was in my mind and on my heart—that I needed to call you and tell you it was time for you to leave that job. And I think it really is time."

"Frank, this is a really high paying, really good job. Why would you tell me to leave it?"

Our conversation continued for another minute or two, with no firm conclusion except that Frank thought it was time for me to leave Cigna, and he didn't know why.

I hung up the phone and said, "Okay, God. I asked for confirmation. This man never gives me advice—refuses to give me advice—and now he's calling me out of the blue and telling me to leave my job. That seems pretty clear to me."

When God wants you to do something that makes no sense to your natural mind, He has a way of really making sure you get it. You still have to trust that He knows what He's doing. You still have to take the step of faith. And you have to stay in faith down the road. But in the moment of decision, He can give you enough confirmation to where you know that what you are experiencing *simply has to be Him* giving you direction for your life.

I walked into the next room where my wife, Debra, was sitting and I announced, "Debra, I'm leaving this job at Cigna."

She almost erupted with joy and relief. "Thank God. Thank God!"

I said, "Debra, I don't have another job yet. I just told you I'm leaving my job and you're happy about that?"

"Yes, Ralph. This is an answer to prayer because the stress on you is too much. I'm scared everyday that I'm going to answer the phone and hear Kathy tell me you've had a heart attack."

She was right. The job was a lot of stress. Probably no more than an executive position with any similar organization. It's just the nature of an executive position for such a large company. There is a lot of responsibility and pressure.

Frank Jr.'s phone call was enough confirmation. But for a married person, God's ultimate confirmation for an important decision will normally come through your spouse. If they're not at peace about what you're wanting to do, you might want to take it back to the Lord in prayer.

In this case, I had heard God leading me in a different direction. I'd gotten confirmation through the eldest male in my family. Then I'd gotten confirmation through my wife.

I turned in my notice the next day, and it would prove to be one of the best decisions of my life.

LANDING MY DREAM JOB

For the next three months, I tried to figure out what to do. Not content to simply sit and do nothing, I started my own little insurance agency. I got a few accounts that were paying me some commissions, and I could have easily done well. The problem is that I was feeling strongly like this is not what I was called to do.

At that time, I was also routinely getting calls from major insurance companies to see if I would be interested in executive positions with them. But I never thought the Lord had led me away from Cigna for any reason to do with that particular company. Instead, I felt strongly that the Lord had something else for me.

One day, I had another one of those unsolicited, out of the blue type of moments. My friend John Covington called and told me that God had prompted him to offer me a job. John is an engineer by trade who owns Chesapeake Consulting, a company that specializes in leadership and workforce development. Back at that time, their primary areas of expertise were manufacturing, technology, and business processes. But they needed someone to help in the area of sales and marketing.

They were actually having so much success in making their clients more productive, that their clients were needing help to sell the extra output they were producing. John is a problem solver by nature, so he saw a problem and prayed for a solution.

I knew this wasn't the calling God had on my life, but this would be an opportunity to help a friend grow his business, to learn some new skills, and to make a positive impact in the world. Sometimes you just have to try things in life. Even if something isn't the perfect long-term fit, it could be exactly what you need for that moment.

ALWAYS MAKING AN IMPACT

The next 18 months or so, I worked to help Chesapeake implement solutions for their clients. In regard to positive impact, there are no dramatic stories about facing off with blatant racists. But there were times when the mere fact of my presence had a positive impact.

We walked into a lot of manufacturing facilities during those 18 months. Manufacturing facilities typically have a clear class structure for their employees. There are the hourly blue-collar workers, and then there are the salaried white-collar professionals.

We would go through tours of these facilities. The blue-collar workers are all busy at their machines and work stations. And then you have the white collar and suited executives walking around. There were some instances when there were plenty of Black people among the blue-collar workers.

But even as late as 2003, there were some facilities that had little or no Black members of management. No Black executives. No Black engineers. No Black plant managers.

On more than one occasion, it was reported back to us that the African American workers were encouraged and inspired to see a Black man walking around with the executive team.

If you are a minority, you can make an impact merely with your presence. Never underestimate how much you can influence the world around you. Recognize that every personal goal you achieve has the power to make a positive impact for your race and for the world at large.

I am very appreciative to John and to Chesapeake for the opportunity they gave me. It made for a positive time of transition in my life, and it would prove to be the last step before landing what turned out to be my dream job.

A NEW CALLING

Back during my time at Cigna, I had sold an insurance contract to the PGA TOUR. When we sold the job, it was another case of a client gushing over how well our team had done in the presentation. Perhaps most noteworthy to them was how well I seemed to understand the game of golf, how well I understood their organization, and how Cigna's offerings were practically a perfect fit with their needs.

So I had made a good impression on the PGA TOUR, and I had kept in contact with some of their people. One day, a guy from their finance department named Ron Price called me up and told me about an affiliate of the PGA TOUR called PGA TOUR Superstore.

The PGA TOUR itself is a business partner, not the owner of the stores. Technically, the PGA TOUR Superstore is a licensee of the PGA TOUR. Ron explained that a former executive of Home Depot had been involved in creating this new company. At that time they were needing help in the area of sales and marketing, and Ron thought I would be perfect for it.

I wasn't convinced it was what I was supposed to do, so Ron said, "Well, look, you need to talk to this guy named Jorge Cora."

Jorge Cora was a member of Atlanta Country Club, and I played golf with him pretty regularly. Now it was starting to seem like maybe something was lining up—maybe this call was for a greater purpose. At Ron's urging, I agreed to talk to Jorge about the opportunity. I pretty much saw him every weekend around the club, so it wouldn't be a big deal to have a conversation about it.

The next time I saw Jorge, I walked up to him and got straight to the point. "Jorge, Ron Price called me. He said you all at PGA TOUR Superstore only have two stores right now, but you have major investment capital and you're about to shoot for explosive growth. He said you're needing help, and he thought I might be able to help somehow."

"Absolutely, yes we need help. Are you available? I didn't know you were available. I'd love for you to come and help us! Come help us, that would be great!"

I said, "I'm not sure yet. I mean, help you do what, exactly?"

He said, "I'm not sure. That's a good question. It's not

really my area. Will you at least come interview with Bill Hamlin, our founder and CEO?"

"Sure, I'll go talk to Bill."

After about twenty minutes of meeting with Bill, he was really interested. "Ralph, I'm really impressed. Your communication skills are excellent. You'll fit right in. Come help us. Come be a part of this."

At this point the CEO and the CFO had both asked me to "come help" their organization. As much as I appreciated their interest in me, I was still not completely sure I could help. They didn't even have a position or a job description yet. They basically just said, "Come help. We'll figure it out. And we'll pay you while we do."

I just said, "Okay." I mean it was kind of like, "Okay? Sure. Why not?"

And again, that has turned out to be one of the best decisions I ever made.

I was already very plugged into the golfing community. I knew marketing. I knew sales. I was good at dealing with people. It did seem to make a lot of sense the more I thought about it.

In December of 2005, I took the job as Director of Corporate Sales for PGA TOUR Superstore. When I came on board, they had just opened their third store. We now have 46 big box retail stores around the country, and our online business dominates the market.

So from a business standpoint, it has been wonderful. I love my job. The people. The industry. It's truly a dream job from a purely personal perspective. It's the type of job that made me almost forget my last career. Even though I spent almost 30 years in the health care business, once I started this new career I never looked back.

GREATER REWARDS

But beyond the personal rewards, this job has something much more meaningful going on with it. During another of my early conversations with Bill Hamlin, when I still had not officially come on board, I told him, "Bill, I don't want to do just a job. I want to do something with purpose. I want to make a difference—to do something that helps people."

Bill perked up, "Ralph, I'm so glad you said that. One of the main purposes of our company is to help people. We're going to be partnering with almost every major charity to put on their golf tournaments. We're going to support them and help maximize the impact of these tournaments. So one of the main things I'll need you to do is build a golf tournament program to help charities."

That's when I knew I had found the right opportunity. Bill had such a big heart for charity. He was formerly an executive with Home Depot, and had come up in that company during the early years with its founders. If you don't know much about them, their whole business is built around the philosophy that you can marry the concept of "doing good" with the concept of "making profits"— something most people thought couldn't be done when these men first set out to prove that it could.

For the last 15 years, my job has involved supporting charity golf tournaments around the country. I get to work closely with many charities to help raise money for worthy causes. This has united my work life with my other major passion in life—to give, serve, and love others well.

WORKING FOR MR. BLANK

In 2010 Arthur Blank, the well-known co-founder of Home Depot and current owner of the Atlanta Falcons, bought out the other investors, becoming the controlling owner of PGA TOUR Superstore. That took the charitable focus of the stores up to an even higher level. I've been privileged to work for Arthur all these years since.

He is one of the most charitable human beings on the planet. As he explains in his recently published book, *Good Company*, giving away money is one of his favorite things to do. But he's not even stingy with his favorite activity. He actually allows me to help support charity programs. In other words, he lets me help give away his money!

As a recent example, we just awarded a $9.5 million grant to the First Tee organization to help build character in teenagers through the game of golf. In addition to the many other programs First Tee already has going, they will now put on a five-week leadership development program to 1,300 youth at PGA TOUR Superstore.

Forty more teens will be chosen to participate in a week-long summit at Arthur's Montana Ranch. All of First Tee's programs are designed to help build honesty, integrity, sportsmanship, and character in young people. I'm very grateful to everyone at PGA TOUR Superstore, especially President and CEO Dick Sullivan, for trusting me to use my gift of building relationships to help develop these programs. Another of our recent efforts involves helping train charities on how to be more effective in their charity work. And I get to be involved with things like that all day, every day.

That part of my job brings blessings that are truly beyond description.

If you ever get the chance to do something you enjoy while at the same time helping other people, consider yourself most blessed.

I know I do.

CONCLUSION

YOU CAN DO WHAT THEY SAY CAN'T
BE DONE

If you can indulge me for just a moment, I'd like to take you back to that meeting with the executives of the largest bank in Florida. The vice president had cornered me at dinner, and was continuing to gush about how effective my presentation had been—something that had shocked him considering I was Black.

He continued his line of questioning, looking for some kind of explanation that would help him process what he was experiencing. He wanted to know how I had gotten so good at my craft, and I just responded truthfully, that it was all about education and preparation.

That's true for anything in life. Just like with athletics, yes, there is natural skill. But the team that works the hardest and puts in the most hours probably has the best chance of winning.

So I always worked the hardest I could, and I hope my example has an influence on young Black people. Here is what I would tell young Black people today: You can do whatever you set your mind to do, and there is still plenty of good land to be taken.

One of the most powerful days of my life as a Black man was the day Barack Obama was sworn in as President of the United States. It's not that I agreed with all of his policies—I didn't.

But what mattered most to me on that day was that it was finally being done. Growing up, our teachers and parents told us, "You can be anything you want to be. You can do anything you want to do. You could even be the President of the United States one day."

Only, that wasn't true. At least it didn't seem true to any Black kid in the 1960s and 70s. In our minds, being president was completely off limits. It just did not seem possible. So as Black children, when someone told us that we could be president, I think most of us did not believe it was true.

Fortunately, one man believed it was true. And he showed everyone else that it was true. It was possible for a Black person to become president. He had fulfilled what many Black parents had told their children for decades. The parents had told the children, "You can take that good land." All it took was for one of the children to actually believe it.

Once you see that it can be done, you start to believe you can do it too. And as a people, we have taken many good, promised lands in the United States. Barack Obama showed that there is no longer any ceiling—there is no barrier that we can't penetrate. But there is still so much more good land to be taken.

Equality remains a long way off, and that means we have plenty more to achieve.

The plight of African Americans in the United States has a lot of parallels to the Israelites and their situation in Egypt, as described in the book of Exodus. The Israelites were under the oppression of slavery in the land of Egypt for hundreds of years. But God heard their cries, and He brought them out of that land.

He led them toward a better land. A land of freedom. A land of prosperity. A land flowing with milk and honey.

When they got there, many of them believed that it would be too hard to take the land. They did not believe that God was with them, and that He would give them the land. It looked like the current inhabitants of the land were much too strong for them, so they were afraid.

But there were two men who said this: "The land we passed through and explored is exceedingly good. If the Lord is pleased with us, he will lead us into that land, a land flowing with milk and honey, and will give it to us" (Numbers 14:7-8 NIV).

Joshua and Caleb believed that they could go in and take this good land because God was with them. And you know what? They are the only two out of their generation who actually got to go in and take the good land.

Our ancestors undoubtedly cried out to the Lord for freedom. For equality. For prosperity.

Those prayers are still before God's throne in Heaven.

We are the beneficiaries of those prayers, and they are still in the process of being answered. But we have to come into agreement with the prayers of those previous generations. We must choose to believe that we can take this promised land.

Unlike the Israelites, we are not called to expel or

exterminate the existing inhabitants of any land. We are called to share this land with the people who are already fully enjoying its benefits.

And to do so—that is our promised land. To forgive the past. Move forward into the future. And experience the fullness of what God has for Black people in America.

You can do it. You can be the first one in your family to graduate college. You can be the first one to own a successful business. Maybe you can be the first Black executive at your company.

Some of the "firsts" in my life may not have seemed all that notable. For example, after being recently elected, I will soon become the first Black president of the Georgia State Golf Association. That "first" probably won't make huge headlines, but time will tell what kind of impact I can have in that role. Even before I step into that particular role, I was already the first Black man to have a scholarship endowed in his name for the Georgia State Golf Association—a first that will definitely benefit people who come after me.

Whatever your first is, set your mind to it, work hard, and achieve it.

Take every opportunity you can, even if they seem small. And continue to dream big. There are still plenty of great achievements yet to be claimed. First Black female president —maybe that's you?

First Black evangelist to see hundreds of thousands of souls saved in the United States, and to lead crusades like Billy Graham? Maybe that's you.

If you can't be the first—because whatever you want to be has already been done—then maybe you can be *one of the first*. It doesn't really matter. What matters is that you look out over your promised land, and you decide to go in and take it. Because you believe in God and you believe in yourself—you believe in what He created you to be.

And you refuse to stop until you get there.

AN INVITATION TO PARADISE

CALLED WRITERS
CHRISTIAN PUBLISHING

All of us wonder why there is pain in the world. We struggle with questions like, "Why would a good God allow so much suffering?" When we ask that question, what we're effectively saying is, "Why doesn't God do something?" We struggle to understand why He doesn't step in and put an end to human suffering once and for all.

The reality is, He is going to do that very thing. One day, He will physically step back into the scene. He is going to put His foot on the Mount of Olives in Jerusalem, and begin the process of restoring earth to its former glory and perfection. The Bible describes the future earth this way:

Then I saw "a new heaven and a new earth," for the first heaven and the first earth had passed away, and there was no longer any sea. I saw the Holy City, the new Jerusalem, coming down out of heaven from God, prepared as a bride beautifully dressed for her husband. And I heard a loud voice from the throne saying, "Look! God's dwelling place is now among the people, and he will dwell with them. They will be his people, and God himself will be with them and be their God. 'He will wipe every tear from their eyes. There will be no more death' or mourning or crying or pain, for the old order of things has passed away."

He who was seated on the throne said, "I am making everything new!"

— REVELATION 21:1-5 NIV

No more tears. No more pain.

The world that we all long for is coming.

It's on the way.

The big question is: Will you be part of that new world?

In order to be part of that new world, we must receive Jesus Christ as Lord and Savior. There will be pleasures beyond anything we can imagine in that new world. In fact, one of the first things we will experience there is a huge party called "The Wedding Feast of the Lamb." There will be wine, music, dancing, celebration, and immense joy.

But there will not be any rebellion against God.

The only people who will be in God's new world will be the ones who chose to love Him and give their lives to Him. Just like Jesus asked His disciples, "Who do you say that I am?" we must all answer that same question.

WHO IS JESUS?

God the Father sent His One and Only Son, Jesus Christ, to this imperfect world to redeem us and restore us into a free and open relationship with Himself. Because humankind had sinned, our relationship with God was broken. Severed. And we were under the penalty of sin, which is punishment and death.

Instead of leaving us to suffer those penalties, Jesus decided to take our place. He took our punishment for us by dying a gruesome death on the cross. Jesus was then buried, and on the third day, He was resurrected into eternal life. He defeated death and the grave, and that means we can now freely receive forgiveness for all of our sins.

GOD'S OFFER TO EVERYONE

Eternal life with God in His perfect world is offered to all of us.

If we choose to reject this offer, that means we are choosing sin over God. We are choosing to stay in rebellion toward Him. This will be the result for those who choose to stay in rebellion toward God:

"But the cowardly, the unbelieving, the vile, the murderers, the sexually immoral, those who practice magic arts, the idolaters and all liars—they will be consigned to the fiery lake of burning sulfur. This is the second death."

— *REVELATION 21:8 NIV*

When presented with options in life, we all want to make the best decision. We weigh all of our important decisions, and we choose carefully.

You can make the right choice today. At this very moment, you are being given the option to end your rebellion toward God, turn away from sin, and choose to receive His forgiveness. You can choose right now to receive Christ as Savior.

A PRAYER FOR SALVATION

If you want to receive Christ as Savior, here is a prayer you can pray right now:

God, I want to live in Heaven with You forever. I do not want to live in sin and rebellion. No human being is perfect, including me. I have done things that You say are wrong. Please forgive me of all my sins, and please give me a new life with You. I now receive Jesus Christ as my Lord and Savior.

Thank You, God, for saving me!

This section of the book is a note from the publisher to share the Gospel of Jesus Christ and invite you, the reader, into a relationship with Him. The reason for this invitation is simple: We want every human being alive to go to Heaven. If you made a decision to receive Christ as Savior today, please reach out to us at CalledWriters.com and let us know.

We want to celebrate with you, and also help you with next steps. God bless you!

RECENT RELEASES FROM CALLED WRITERS

CALLED WRITERS
CHRISTIAN PUBLISHING

THE
Jericho
FAST

How to Break through Walls
with Prayer and Fasting

RHODA FAYE DIEHL

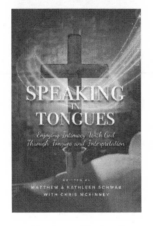

SPEAKING
IN
TONGUES

*Enjoying Intimacy With God
Through Tongues and Interpretation*

WRITTEN BY
MATTHEW & KATHLEEN SCHWAB
WITH CHRIS MCKINNEY

NOTES

1. THE END OF SEGREGATED ATHLETICS

1. "B.T. Washington Montgomery Yellow Jackets," AHSFHS.org, Alabama High School Football Historical Society.
2. Ibid
3. Wikipedia, "Cramton Bowl," wikipedia.com, https://en.wikipedia.org/wiki/Cramton_Bowl

2. THE CALL OF INTEGRATION

1. Correction notice: Earlier copies of the book incorrectly indicated that these players would be "the first" Black players. There actually was a single Black player named Joe Berry who had played on special teams in the prior year. This was a mistake of the publisher during editing, and not the mistake of the primary author. We deeply regret the error.
2. "Jim Chafin," AHSFHS.org, http://www.ahsfhs.org/Coaches/coachestop.asp?Coach=Jim%20Chafin
3. Chasing the Frog, "Remember the Titans (2000)," chasingthefrog.com, http://www.chasingthefrog.com/reelfaces/rememberthetitans.php

3. INTEGRATION COSTS SOMETHING

1. Powell, William J. (1934). Black Wings. Los Angeles: Ivan Deach, Jr.

4. MAJOR INFLUENCES

1. Lynn McMillon, "Fred Gray on injustice and his hope for the church," christianchronicle.org, https://christianchronicle.org/fred-gray-on-injustice-and-his-hope-for-the-church/

7. RACIAL PROBLEMS AT ALABAMA

1. Jerry Blackwell, "From Play-Action to Legal Action: Rick Davis," si.com, https://www.si.com/college/alabama/bamacentral/where-are-they-now-ricky-davis-Blackwell

11. BLACK IS NOT A LIABILITY

1. Alex Scarborough, "DeVonta Smith's long climb from skinny recruit to Heisman Trophy winner," espn.com, https://www.espn.com/college-football/story/_/id/30113109/devonta-smith-long-climb-skinny-recruit-heisman-trophy-winner

13. AMERICA'S COUNTRY CLUBS: BLACK GOLFERS NEED NOT APPLY

1. "Shoal Creek racism storm: Looking back at controversy around 1990 PGA," Sky Sports, https://www.skysports.com/golf/news/12176/12046141/shoal-creek-racism-storm-looking-back-at-controversy-around-1990-pga
2. Readers can access a copy of the article at this URL: https://www.newspapers.com/newspage/403892811/

ABOUT THE CO-AUTHOR

Chris McKinney is the founder and managing editor of Called Writers Christian Publishing. He is honored to have the opportunity to write, edit, rewrite, and co-author many Christian books.

Chris's ministry articles have been published by *CBN, Crosswalk, Engage Magazine,* and many other publications and websites. He was formerly the executive editor of *GODSPEED Magazine,* where he had the privilege of serving under David Aikman, a legendary Christian journalist and bestselling author. Chris has also been a featured guest on various Christian radio, internet, and television shows.

ABOUT THE AUTHOR

Ralph Stokes was a key player on the southern football scene during the time of integration. After college, he was a pioneer for integration in the insurance industry. He is currently the Director of Partnership Marketing for PGA TOUR Superstore and President-Elect of the Georgia State Golf Association. Ralph is very passionate about partnering with and supporting different charities across the United States. Ralph lives in Atlanta, Georgia, with his wife, Debra. They have two daughters and two granddaughters.

in

Made in the USA
Middletown, DE
18 September 2022

10602115R00137